LOOSE PARTS 2

11/2017

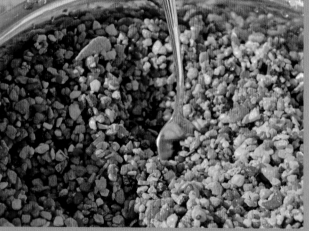

Other Redleaf Press Books by Lisa Daly and Miriam Beloglovsky

Loose Parts
Inspiring Play in Young Children

Early Learning Theories Made Visible

Loose Parts 2

INSPIRING PLAY WITH INFANTS AND TODDLERS

Lisa Daly and Miriam Beloglovsky ■ Photography by Jenna Daly

Redleaf Press®
www.redleafpress.org
800-423-8309

Published by Redleaf Press
10 Yorkton Court
St. Paul, MN 55117
www.redleafpress.org

First edition 2016
Cover design by Jim Handrigan
Cover and interior photographs by Jenna Daly
Interior design by Erin Kirk New
Typeset in Berkeley Oldstyle Book
Printed in the United States of America

The "Types and Presentation of Loose Parts to Provide" section of chapter 1 first
appeared in "Introducing Loose Parts to Preschoolers" by Lisa Daly and Miriam
Beloglovsky. 2015. *Teaching Young Children*. Washington, D.C.: NAEYC. Reprinted
with permission from the National Association for the Education of Young
Children (NAEYC): vol. 9, no. 1, pp. 18–20.

Library of Congress Cataloging-in-Publication Data

Names: Beloglovsky, Miriam, author. | Daly, Lisa, author.
Title: Loose parts 2 : inspiring play with infants and toddlers / Miriam
    Beloglovsky and Lisa Daly ; photography by Jenna Daly.
Other titles: Loose parts two
Description: First edition. | St. Paul, MN : Redleaf Press, 2016.
Identifiers: LCCN 2016003405 (print) | LCCN 2016006433 (ebook) | ISBN
    9781605544649 (paperback : alk. paper) | ISBN 9781605544656 (ebook)
Subjects: LCSH: Play. | Early childhood education--Activity programs. |
    Creative activities and seat work. | BISAC: EDUCATION / Teaching Methods &
    Materials / General. | FAMILY & RELATIONSHIPS / Life Stages / Infants &
    Toddlers. | EDUCATION / Curricula. | EDUCATION / Classroom Management.
Classification: LCC LB1139.35.P55 B45 2016 (print) | LCC LB1139.35.P55
    (ebook) | DDC 372.21--dc23
LC record available at http://lccn.loc.gov/2016003405

U16-08

To all who value infants and toddlers as capable and competent

To all who view infants and toddlers as active researchers

To all who see infants and toddlers as protagonists of their own learning

To all who see loose parts as treasures

To all who dare to wonder

Contents

Acknowledgments

Many dear friends, family members, colleagues, and early childhood educators have provided us with inspiration and significant support throughout the writing and photographing of this book. We value the collaborative relationships that we have built during this project and would like to acknowledge the following individuals and programs for their contributions.

To our family and friends, we thank you for your continued support and help in finding and collecting intriguing loose parts—from palm tree stumps and Kentucky coffee pods to colorful baby food jar caps—as well as in transforming loose parts into captivating play experiences, such as sound gardens, for infants and toddlers. Thank you for putting up with us as we worked long hours.

We are indebted to so many of the staff at KidZKount in Auburn, California, which has offered child services for over fifty years, enriched children's lives, and transformed families. Denyse Cardoza, executive director, KidZKount: We are grateful for your vision, extraordinary support, professionalism, and leadership. Victoria Treadway, preschool child development specialist: We are appreciative of your understanding, care, dedication, and passion for young children and teachers. Anne Wolf, infant/toddler child development specialist: Thank you for coming in and embracing classroom transformations and intentional teaching, learning, and reflection. Linda Sandoval, family services coordinator: Thank you for partnering with us to support and strengthen family relationships and engagement.

Dr. Annie White, assistant professor of early childhood studies, California State University Channel Islands, has significantly impacted our lives. Annie, thank you for your commitment, integrity, and passion, and most importantly for being a reflective partner and helping us see infants in a deeper, more profound way.

Jenna Daly, thank you for your ability to capture amazing photographs and for your organizational support and assistance. Most importantly, we acknowledge your remarkable ability to engage with children and advocate for what is best for them. You have made many friends in the process.

The teachers at Baby Steps (Loomis Early Head Start) welcomed us into their learning environment and supported our infusion of loose parts into their classrooms. To Lindsey Shafer, Janna Johnson, Sara Feiling, Sharla Klopp, and Stacey Green, we give an enormous thank-you for allowing us to photograph your extraordinary environment, for being receptive and eager to try new ideas, and for engaging in the journey with us. Carson and Calliope, thank you for allowing us to photograph Opi, our incredible model.

Our sincere gratitude goes to Cheri Quishenbery, who opened up her home child care in Lincoln, California, and enthusiastically embraced loose parts. Cheri, thank you for your creativity and eagerness to engage with us in this process. You always surpass our expectations.

Solano Community College in Solano, California, was instrumental in allowing us to capture their captivating infant and toddler outdoor environment. Our gratitude goes to Christie Speck, children's program director, for warmly welcoming us and permitting us to photograph. Juwan Vartanian, children's program specialist, you are an inspiration. Juwan, the outdoor environments you create for infants and toddlers are abundant in natural materials and rich in play possibilities, and they provoke curiosity and wonder. Thank you for your passion.

We want to express our thanks to the children and families of Baby Steps, Cheri Quishenbery's home child care, and Solano Community College for permitting us to capture your children's learning stories. It was a delight and pleasure getting to know your children and observing their experiments, investigations, and relationships.

This book could not have happened without the vision, support, technical expertise, and creative efforts of everyone at Redleaf Press. Special appreciation goes out to David Heath, director of Redleaf Press, for believing in us; Kara Lomen, acquisitions and developmental editor, for her support and editing knowledge; and Laurie Buss Herrmann, content development manager, for her understanding when we have gone through writer's burnout.

LOOSE PARTS 2

Part 1
Introduction to Loose Parts for Infants and Toddlers

Infants and toddlers are natural scientists with an intrinsic drive to investigate and master their world. Play with loose parts fosters even the youngest children's sense of wonder and curiosity as they explore the potential of intriguing, unexpected, upcycled, and natural materials.

When loose parts are introduced to infants and toddlers, rich, magnificent explorations transpire. Astonishing learning and unexpected capabilities are revealed as the youngest of children make sense of their world. Accidental occurrences become significant and visible as caregivers thoughtfully observe children's engagement with materials, reflect on the importance of the interactions, and respectfully respond to children's intentions. Infants and toddlers are researchers who are fascinated by the properties of objects and how things work. They explore materials with all of their senses and delight in cause-and-effect relationships. Loose parts are captivating objects for infants and toddlers to investigate because of their open-ended nature. Loose parts allow young children to be in control of their inquiries as they gather and learn information about physical objects.

Safety   Drawing on inspiration from *Loose Parts: Inspiring Play in Young Children*, this sequel highlights loose parts that are particularly appropriate for infants and toddlers. We selected the loose parts featured in this book specifically for use with young children under the age of three. Every material represented in this book has been infant and toddler tested and teacher reviewed for safety. Even so, we caution that young children should never be left unattended with any of the objects. Supervision of children by observant adults is critical and always the best safety prevention.

So, what's the same about this book and its predecessor, *Loose Parts: Inspiring Play in Young Children*? Both books:

- provide a science-based context for how play with loose parts supports young children's development and learning;
- explain the value of loose parts;
- include beautiful and inspiring photographs;
- contain captivating stories of young children's explorations with loose parts;
- suggest creative ideas for discovery and investigation;
- offer new uses for upcycled materials; and
- reveal how to integrate loose parts into children's play and environment.

And what's different? This book:

- focuses on infants and toddlers under the age of three rather than preschool-age children;
- utilizes loose parts that meet the safety, feature, and function needs of infants and toddlers;
- presents a variety of new and innovative loose parts ideas;
- includes photographs taken in engaging infant/toddler early learning environments; and
- is organized according to play-action characteristics (such as grasping, banging, filling, and stacking) of infants and toddlers.

CHAPTER 1
What Are Loose Parts?

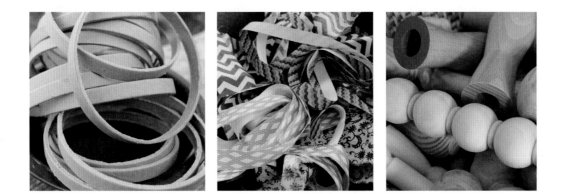

The term *loose parts* was originally coined by British architect Simon Nicholson to describe open-ended materials that can be used and manipulated in different ways (Nicholson 1971). He believed that every human being has the potential to be creative and that loose parts in an environment invite immense imaginative possibilities unlikely in settings with fixed elements. As researchers, scientists, and educators recognize the potential of loose parts in promoting learning and development in young children, an increasing number of early childhood classrooms today are incorporating a wide variety of loose parts into their environments.

Loose parts are captivating, open-ended, and mobile objects that are intriguing and fascinating to infants and toddlers. The youngest of children find loose parts to be irresistible and appealing. Innately curious, infants and toddlers are attracted toward objects that are enticing and novel, such as cardboard tubes, spoons, stones, seashells, and scarves. Young children become deeply engaged as they explore objects through their senses. Each item makes distinctive sounds, moves differently, and has interesting textures, varying weights, and multiple colors. Motto, ten months old, has been mouthing a variety of spoons and discovering that each spoon has its own unique smell, color, taste, and texture. Leonardo, sixteen months old, has been drawn to a basket of balls. He learns that balls move differently when thrown or rolled. He looks surprised when he grasps one ball and hears a jingling sound. Leonardo discovers that the ball makes a different sound when he grasps it tightly or loosely.

Loose parts are open-ended materials that have unlimited play possibilities. They have multiple rather than single outcomes, which means that there is not a specific way to use items. A plastic musical toy is a closed object that has one intent: sound is made as an infant pushes a button. Toy manufacturers claim that infants will be delighted by its vivid colors, fascinating texture, and engaging sounds. The reality is that the novelty of such a toy wears off very quickly. Once a young child has mastered the single task of making a sound, he is ready to move on to another challenge. Loose parts, however, are adaptable and provide young children with infinite play possibilities. Infants use their senses to investigate loose parts to discover intriguing aspects such as texture or sound. For instance, nine-month-old Jesenia grasps an extra-large button and brings it up to her mouth. Later she drops buttons into a coconut shell and bangs a button on a metal door frame, seeming interested in the sounds made by her actions. Toddlers' play becomes more complex as they build the capacity of symbolic function, which includes the ability to use objects to stand for something else. Addy, twenty-two months old, uses a green ball as an apple, and Marlysa, twenty-two months old, uses bark as coffee. Balls and bark are open-ended materials as they lend themselves to various uses.

Loose parts are mobile objects that can be carried and moved from one place to another. Young children regularly are interested in transporting items in pockets, buckets, baskets, and bags. Offering loose parts and a variety of containers supports toddlers' intense desire to transport. Jacob, twelve months old, pushes a dump truck loaded with pinecones to the sand area, and Samuel and Addy, older toddlers, collect stones and transport them to their playhouse. Saige is a toddler who has not been walking for very long. She fills a bucket with foot-long metal chains and carries the heavy load across the play yard. In each instance, mobility is an important attribute of loose parts, as young children naturally move open-ended objects and use them for self-directed play.

Loose parts are beautiful, alluring materials that captivate children and are known for their significant play value. Loose parts may be used in multiple ways by young children, but they are substantially more than open-ended objects. They are part of an educational philosophy embraced by teachers for their power to transform early childhood learning environments and provoke meaningful play experiences. Loose parts, and organizational materials for storing and displaying them, come in a wide assortment, from a variety of intriguing sources, and may be found, free, repurposed, or purchased inexpensively.

Types of Loose Parts

Loose parts can be made of many different materials, such as wood, metal, plastic, glass, fabric, or paper, or they can be objects from nature.

When incorporating loose parts for infants into your environment, consider appropriate items that invite action and opportunity for babies to touch,

mouth, explore, move, bang, and rearrange. Examples include balls, knotted cloth napkins, hair rollers, and bracelets. For toddlers, select items that they may transform, transport, and construct. When a toddler plays with a plastic apple, it is always an apple, but when she plays with a pinecone, she may choose for it to represent an apple, a tree, or a ball for rolling—anything that she imagines. Toddlers love to fill, dump, and carry things, so provide materials to support these interests, such as coasters, large glass stones, rocks, postcards, and scarves. Also add materials with interesting properties that can be used for design or construction, or be made into props. Natural, found, and upcycled objects such as seashells, stones, tiles, ribbon, and fabric are some examples.

Choking Hazard

When selecting loose parts for the environment, teachers need to ensure that the parts are large and sturdy enough not to be a choking hazard. A choke test cylinder is a tool used to determine whether an item is the appropriate size. Balancing supervision with safeguards will help prevent accidents while allowing infants and toddlers to explore.

Found and Free Materials

Loose parts may be found materials. Nature hikes or your own backyard yield natural loose parts, such as leaves, rocks, pinecones, bamboo, tree stumps, or driftwood. Weekend adventures can provide some of the best loose parts finds, including free wooden cable spools and wood scraps from a hardware store for

construction; cardboard cove molding at a home furnishing store to be used as ramps; car tires from a tire shop for climbing on; or picture frame molding or matting from a frame shop for design.

Upcycled Materials

Upcycled materials, repurposed for another use, support loose parts play in infants and toddlers. Examples include using a wine rack as a stand to support cove molding, metal napkin rings for sound exploration, or a colander for inserting pipe cleaners. You can also upcycle unexpected materials from your own home to use with young children, such as carpet tubes found in the garage; plastic clothes hangers from a closet; cooking utensils found in drawers; or fabric in cabinets.

Thrift stores and garage sales yield a multitude of loose parts, from potato mashers and baskets to wooden bowls. Once family members and friends learn about loose parts, they excitedly begin to save items such as unused picture frames or colorful plastic bottle caps and contribute to teachers' collections. The possibilities in working with young children and loose parts are endless.

Purchased Materials

Discount stores offer a wide variety of loose parts that may be purchased at a minimal cost. Items include colorful plastic cups and containers for light investigations, loofahs to explore texture, large glass stones for transporting, and knotted tug ropes for grasping.

Why Loose Parts for Infants and Toddlers Are Important

Infants and toddlers learn heuristically, that is, through investigating, discovering, or problem solving by experimental and trial-and-error methods. Therefore, it is important for teachers and caregivers to provide open-ended materials (loose parts) that allow infants and toddlers opportunity to explore their properties and functions.

In *From Neurons to Neighborhoods*, Shonkoff and Phillips identify the core concept that "children are active participants in their own development, reflecting the intrinsic human drive to explore and master one's environment" (2000, 27). Infants and toddlers need opportunities to learn about the world by engaging in meaningful learning experiences. Their investigation happens with their senses as they mouth items and manipulate things with their hands. Loose parts stimulate young children's sense of touch, sound, sight, and smell, and can be

used in a variety of ways. For instance, children can fill and dump, transport, collect, mix, connect, take apart, line up, and stack loose parts. Because the possibilities with loose parts are endless, each age group, infants and toddlers, use the same materials in ways that are appropriate for their developmental level.

Loose parts support the dynamic and multidimensional nature of young children's learning. Children of all ages, abilities, skill levels, and genders can use loose parts successfully. Because there's no right or wrong way to work with these items, infants and toddlers may use them according to their ability and interest. For example, a young infant may look at, feel, grasp, and mouth a large, polished tile sample; a mobile infant may stack the tiles; and an older toddler may fill a bucket with them and then dump them out.

Magda Gerber, world-renowned child therapist and infant specialist, developed a philosophy of treating infants with respect and trust in their abilities to develop naturally and at their own pace. Her approach revolutionized infant/toddler care and set the standard for high-quality care and early childhood education. In her teachings, Gerber addresses the importance of young children actively engaging with loose parts, which she calls "play objects," rather than being entertained by passive objects such as mobiles or push-button toys. Open-ended materials are critical in infant and toddler play because they allow children to be in control and to recognize the power of their bodies and actions. Loose parts promote the active learning in infants and toddlers advocated by Magda Gerber, as well as the child's need to manipulate his environment, to experiment, and to interact with materials in order to learn emphasized in Piaget's theory. When young children play with loose parts, they are in charge of making objects move or roll, which helps them make connections to their abilities and influences on their environment. "The best play objects for babies are those which allow them to be as active and competent as possible at every stage of development" (Gerber 2013).

Loose parts deepen critical thinking in infants and toddlers as they explore, examine, hypothesize, and challenge all types of situations, concerns, and information. Alvin, twenty-one months old, attempts to roll a ball down a black gutter propped against a child-size bench. He sits on the bench with a basket of balls placed at the far side of the gutter's base. Alvin's body impedes his ability to reach the balls. Each time he stretches his left hand across his body to grasp a ball, the gutter shifts and falls off the bench. Alvin places the gutter back in position and reaches again. He persists at repeating his actions three times with the same result. He seems to focus on the gutter rather than his body's position. He continues, but this time he grasps a ball with his right hand. The gutter remains in place and Alvin drops the ball with his right hand in the gutter's trough. Alvin repeatedly picks up balls with his right hand, places them at the gutter's top, and watches as the balls roll swiftly down. His ability to solve his problem requires a high level of critical thinking. Young children's problem-solving skills are enhanced by loose parts because exploration is how children build knowledge of the objects in the world around them. When we introduce multiple loose parts that can be moved, manipulated, and made into different things with diverse meanings, children develop higher levels of critical thinking.

Divergent thinking is the ability to generate new ideas and is an important factor in problem solving and innovation. In a research study about differences in divergent thinking in toddlers and preschoolers, Bijvoet–van den Berg and Hoicka (2014) discovered that two-year-olds can think divergently and that children's divergent thinking increases with age. Contributing to divergent thinking is children's use of individual learning to acquire knowledge about novel objects. Therefore, when young children engage in self-directed play with loose parts, they have more opportunity to produce original actions with the materials. Loose parts are unusual objects that offer infinite play prospects, and their lack of script and structure allows children to make them what their imagination dictates. They can be adapted and directed in many ways, which encourages a child's creativity and imagination.

Safety and Loose Parts

Loose parts for infants and toddlers require special considerations when it comes to safety. Because loose parts are generally found materials, extra precaution is needed to assess their size, durability, and age appropriateness. Additionally, safety issues change as infants progress into toddlerhood, so teachers need to know specific safety concerns for each age group when selecting which loose parts to place in the environment. For example, small objects are a choking concern with infants, while tripping over items and pulling heavy objects on top of oneself are more of a concern for older infants and toddlers.

Adult Supervision

Nothing will prevent childhood accidents better than careful adult supervision. An attentive, responsive adult is essential for keeping young children safe and protecting them from injuries. Teachers are responsible for making certain that loose parts placed in the classroom environment are safe for the infants and toddlers who will use them and also for having a watchful eye as the children manipulate the objects. Prevention is key. It is best to foresee and prevent rather than handle an emergency. Experienced teachers, even when working one on one with a child, will always be alert to the whole classroom.

Size

The biggest safety concern with loose parts and infants and toddlers (under twenty-four months) is the size of objects. No small items that are potential choking hazards should be left within a child's reach or used without adult supervision in an early learning environment. Play materials must be large enough that they cannot be swallowed. Small-object choking testers, which may be purchased from a variety of commercial sites, are the best way to measure the size of a loose part. If a piece fits entirely inside the tube, it is considered a choking hazard for children under age three. The United States Consumer Product Safety Commission (www.cpsc.gov; accessed August 2015) states that smooth round objects present the highest risk of choking. If a choke test cylinder is not available, using a toilet paper roll is a quick and easy alternative way to determine if size is appropriate. Any item that fits inside the roll is too small. The size of loose parts becomes less of an issue with older toddlers (twenty-four to thirty-six months) as they rarely mouth play objects; however, adults still need to carefully supervise children's play.

Durability

Upcycled materials need to be carefully checked for sharp edges and loose pieces. Loose parts need to be sturdy and free from small pieces that are not securely attached or small, removable parts that can be broken off and then swallowed or inhaled. Also, inspect materials for peeling paint and ensure that they are not breakable.

Harmful Substances

Infants explore by putting everything in their mouths, so it is important to avoid loose parts that may contain harmful products. The danger from toxic elements is greater in young children than adults because their bodies are smaller and they are still developing. Loose parts may contain chemicals such as lead, phthalates, or polyvinyl chloride (PVC) that have been linked to health problems. Use discretion when selecting loose parts, because many do not come with chemical labels. If at all in doubt, do not use with children.

Age Appropriateness

Commercial toys frequently come with a "recommended age," which is not the case for loose parts. For teachers, the issue of appropriateness involves knowing the children in their care. For instance, if an infant is in a throwing phase, temporarily remove heavy loose parts that may harm others if rocketed, and replace them with softer items for throwing. A loose part that is appropriate for one child may not be okay for another.

Cleanliness/Sanitation

Since infants repeatedly put objects in their mouths, effective cleaning, sanitizing, and disinfecting are regular occurrences in early learning environments to reduce the risk of illness. Follow the same sanitation principles with loose parts as with all other play objects. Choose materials you can scrub, wash, and rinse. An added bonus with loose parts is that since they are free, upcycled, and found materials, they may be thrown away or recycled without worry.

Loose Parts Support Learning and Development across the Domains

Learning and development for infants and toddlers is an integrated process that includes social-emotional, perceptual-motor, cognitive, and language development as young children actively strive to make sense of their world. Maguire-Fong describes infant and toddler learning as a dynamic system in which every-day experiences influence how the child organizes body and mind (2015). Loose parts are ordinary objects filled with opportunities to build life skills, including collaboration, self-knowledge, risk taking, critical thinking, communication, and decision making. Building these skills allows infants and toddlers to grow across each of the developmental domains.

Social-Emotional Learning and Development

Play with loose parts promotes social-emotional development, including self-knowledge, self-regulation, self-esteem, and social skills as infants and toddlers get to know themselves and others.

SELF-KNOWLEDGE

Self-knowledge includes a child's understanding of his own body, abilities, and feelings. An infant first begins to make sense of his world through his senses of touch, sight, taste, hearing, and smell, and through movement. As young children explore intriguing loose parts that are made available to them, they use their senses and movement in new ways, developing an awareness of their own capabilities.

Micco, ten months old, reaches for a silicone baking mold, closes his fingers around it, and directs it to his mouth. He changes body positions frequently as he investigates the mold with his fingers and mouth. Later he grasps a wooden thread spool and a ball, each of which required a different grasping technique. He begins to realize that he can get objects, examine them, and make things happen by using different strategies. Samuel uses all his strength to push a large-diameter corrugated drainage pipe across the lawn, climbs on top of and through tires, and rotates a salad spinner. Each of these movements helps him gain body awareness as he explores objects in his environment.

Children's self-knowledge through their expression of emotions is also exhibited while engaged with loose parts. For instance, Calli, thirty-three months old, looks aggravated when a postcard does not nest neatly into the envelope sorter. She rotates the card in different directions in an attempt to make it fit, but the card continues to extend beyond the slot. Adam exhibits joy and satisfaction as he successfully places a final tree cookie (a cross section of a tree branch or trunk) on top of a tower without it collapsing. Alvin's face reveals his uncertainty when the ball does not roll out of the black irrigation pipe onto the grass. Yoli shows excitement and intensity as she bangs a metal tin in rhythmic strokes with a wooden spoon. She expresses surprise as she accidently hits a wooden bowl with her spoon and hears a deeper, duller sound. She hits the metal can again as if to make certain the tin sound did not disappear.

SELF-REGULATION

Self-regulation involves infants' and toddlers' ability to gain control of bodily functions, manage powerful emotions, and maintain focus and attention (Shonkoff and Phillips 2000). The development of self-regulation is seen in all developmental areas as young children gain control emotionally, socially, physically, and cognitively.

Children become deeply involved and interested, even in the presence of distractions, when they have interesting loose parts to examine and manipulate. Having sufficient time to investigate play objects allows infants and toddlers the ability to fully experience and dictate how to play. The open-ended nature of loose parts allows for multiple play possibilities, such as carrying, stacking, banging, or collecting, thus offering a child the opportunity to regulate her play as she desires, which is not the case with a single-purpose manufactured toy. Self-chosen play with loose parts fosters children's capacity to control their environment.

Alvin, twenty-one months old, stays absorbed at the outside water table for over sixty minutes. He begins by immersing cloth napkins into the soapy water, pushing the napkins underwater, and then pulling them up. His interest shifts multiple times during the hour. He pours and stirs the water, and dunks a plastic salad spinner underwater and then watches water rain down when he picks it up. Occasionally other children come and go from the water table, but Alvin stays engrossed. His actions demonstrate his development of self-regulation as he attends to the water play even when distracted by other children and activity.

SELF-ESTEEM

Self-esteem is an individual's perception of their own worth. It develops as children master new abilities, experience success, and realize their effectiveness. Self-esteem and feelings of efficacy develop as young children take initiative and conquer challenges. Pride in their accomplishments and development of independence may be seen in exploratory play with loose parts when infants and toddlers engage with objects and interesting things happen as a result of their actions.

Julian, nine months old, has just developed the ability to crawl. His teacher invites him to crawl by placing large loose parts into the environment. He crawls on pillows, through tunnels, up and down inclines, and in and out of cardboard boxes. He smiles with delight at his new proficiency, as if to say, "Look what I can do!" Each exploration, freely selected, contributes to the child's sense of competence and achievement.

Toddlers thrive on choices. Nothing gives young children a higher sense of power than being in control of the materials they are using. Because loose parts are open-ended, they allow children the opportunity to make choices and decisions. When working with loose parts, infants and toddlers have power over their environment, as is the case with Adam, who chooses to propel balls off the play loft, knock over all the yarn spools, and jump off tree stumps.

SOCIAL DEVELOPMENT

Social development is a young child's ability to form and maintain healthy and rewarding relationships with adults and other children. An environment organized with appealing loose parts plays a major role in supporting social play in young children. Loose parts that are multiple in number are engaging and offer choices help promote socialization in infants and toddlers.

Toddlers can be intent on having the same play object that someone else has, especially popular items. Loose parts are duplicates of the same items, so conflict and waiting among children is automatically minimized. For example, a wide variety of metal spoons are set up as a *provocation* (intentionally placing intriguing, challenging, or surprising materials in the environment as a way to provoke children's thinking) in Janna's classroom. Adam, Bryce, Lonzo, and Arianna are all captivated with them. Because the number of spoons is plentiful, each child can take several at a time for their investigations of dropping, banging, lining up, batting, transporting, pushing, and stirring.

Collections of loose parts have fascinating characteristics of color, shape, texture, pattern, and design that capture the interest of young children. Their open-ended nature allows them to be used in limitless ways and shared with others. Rather than competition, collaboration is promoted when children interact with loose parts, because there is not a right or wrong way to use them. The metal spoons in Janna's classroom are used in multiple ways. Lonzo is enthralled with the sounds a spoon can make when it is scraped against a wooden bowl, tapped on a metal container, and banged on the inside of a bowl. His pounding becomes contagious, and other children join in the music making. The movement of the spoons rivets Bryce. He stretches his fist grip of spoons up high and then releases them in between the mirrored wall and the indoor climbing ladder. Adam follows Bryce's lead, and the two of them drop spoons in gleeful unison.

Perceptual-Motor Learning and Development

As infants and toddlers engage with loose parts, they are continuously investigating and experimenting to make sense of how their world works. They learn about texture as they touch scratchy loofas, soft blankets, and smooth plastic bowls. They investigate gravity by rolling a ball down an incline or dropping it from up high. Play with loose parts promotes gross-motor skills, fine-motor skills, and hand-eye coordination.

GROSS-MOTOR SKILLS

Gross-motor skills are evident when children climb on pillows or up ramps, pick up heavy tree cookies with both arms, and chase balls. Balance develops as young children walk across logs, stepping-stones, tree trunk borders, or a wood plank bridged between tires. Transporting items and filling/dumping are large-motor skills repeated frequently by toddlers. It's important to have containers in the environment, such as bags, buckets, and crates, along with smaller loose parts that children can fill, transport, dump, and refill. Tree blocks, pinecones, small floor samples (tile, carpet, wood), coasters, and napkin rings make good small loose parts, and sand, water, and clay are natural loose parts.

FINE-MOTOR SKILLS

Fine-motor skills include control and accuracy of actions made with the small muscles of the hands. Small-motor skills increase when infants and toddlers grasp a knotted rope, carefully use their index finger and thumb in a pincer grasp

to pick up a cedar ring, or clip round peg wood clothespins onto a metal bucket. Pouring is supported when young children use cups and containers for pouring water or birdseed. Play with loose parts supports the development of other fine-motor skills, such as moving a small cup from hand to hand, making mud pies and cakes, dropping and picking up bracelets, and banging a spoon on a metal pot.

HAND-EYE COORDINATION

Hand-eye coordination is the integrated ability to use the hands as guided by information from the eyes. It can be seen as Micco, ten months old, brings a wooden cooking utensil to his mouth or Ethan, an older toddler, inserts pipe cleaners in the holes of a colander or pours water into a funnel.

Nine-month-old Jesenia lies on her stomach on her sheepskin rug. She looks inquisitively as her teacher places plastic hair rollers just beyond her grasp. The colorful rollers capture her interest. She starts to pivot her body, reaches for the rollers, and examines them to see how they work. Makayla, twenty-seven months old, uses visual input from her eyes to guide her hands and the fine motor skills of her fingers to twist and unscrew the jar lids and pour water. Calli's eyes watch her fingers work together as she scoops up large glass stones on the light table and then draws in the sand with a piece of driftwood.

Cognitive Learning and Development

Intellectual, or cognitive, learning includes the abilities of predicting, reasoning, questioning, and analyzing. The process of intellectual learning takes place through natural interaction with real things in the child's environment (Katz 2015). Loose parts are real things, ordinary objects, that when placed intentionally in infants' and toddlers' environment, support their cognitive growth through exciting discoveries. According to Gopnik, Meltzoff, and Kuhl, "Childhood is the time when we learn most and when our brains as well as our minds are most open to new experience. . . . Babies and young children are perpetually exploring and experimenting, testing out new theories and changing old theories when they learn something new" (1999, 189).

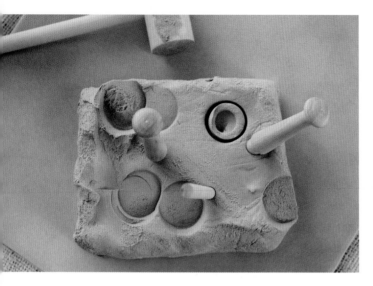

Infants and toddlers have a natural desire to explore the properties of objects, so exposing them to open-ended play with loose parts allows for experimentation and fosters higher-level thinking. Loose parts are the tools of scientists, engineers, artists, and architects. An early childhood environment filled with loose parts is a laboratory that supports a young child's drive to invent and discover, a catalyst for rich problem solving.

Yoli, thirty-three months old, finds working with clay to be a lot of fun. She uses a wooden mallet to pound a hollow cylinder into the wet, pliable clay. The clay becomes stuck inside the cylinder, and she is tested to figure out how to remove it. How will she work to solve the problem? She tries a variety of strategies in her efforts to remove the clay, including shaking the tube, pounding it on the table, and trying to use the mallet head to push it. Ian, who is standing close to Yoli, hands her a dowel. Yoli inserts the dowel into the cylinder and slowly pushes the clay out. Problem solved.

Cognitive development is concerned more with how young children learn rather than what they learn. It involves concept development of causality, classification, seriation, representation of experiences and ideas, number concepts, and spatial relations. According to theorist Jean Piaget (1952), children construct their own knowledge out of direct experiences.

Lonzo, twenty-one months old, matches a jar lid to a container, but the lid is too big. He then uses a strategy of randomly placing different-sized lids on top of the jar. At this time he seems more fascinated with connecting lids and containers than finding a perfect fit. A short while later, he walks past a basket of colorful caps. He selects a purple cap, carries it over to the basket of containers, and places the cap on the container. The purple cap is a bottle cap rather than a lid and does not have grooves for twisting. Lonzo looks at the cap and the container as if to say, "It is a lid, so it should fit on a container." Eventually his experience will lead to immediate identification of matching caps and containers without trial and error.

CAUSALITY

Causality is the ability to notice relationships between cause and effect. Infants and toddlers move from unintentional to intentional actions as they learn to produce an activity that has an effect. Nine-month-old Jesenia demonstrates that she knows the connection between an action (cause) and its outcome (effect) when she shakes a small gourd and it makes a sound, or when she strokes the wheel with her palm and the caster spins.

Adam, twenty-two months old, is also developing causality. He has learned that he is too short with his outstretched hand to touch long ribbons suspended from the ceiling. But he discovers that if he takes a cardboard tube off the shelf and bats the ribbon, it will sway. These experiences demonstrate how both children are building an understanding of causality through the use of loose parts.

CLASSIFICATION

Classification refers to the ability to recognize differences. Infants and toddlers build the ability to identify similarities and differences and categorize as they engage with a wide variety of loose parts. As they handle materials, they learn about attributes such as color, shape, size, texture, and function. For instance, they learn pom-poms are soft, wooden spools are hard, pinecones are prickly, and glass stones are smooth.

Leonardo discovers that the ball and cylinder roll but the cube does not. With experience, young children will begin to cluster like materials together, as with Diego, who separates tiles by placing red tiles in one pile and yellow tiles in another, or Ian, who groups natural materials according to seedpods, nuts, leaves, and pinecones.

SERIATION

Seriation is the concept that materials can be arranged in a logical order according to their differences, such as driftwood pieces from shortest to longest or paint swatches from lightest to darkest. "Infants build the concept of seriation as they notice how objects vary in size and line them up or stack them" (Maguire-Fong 2015, 81). The same is true for toddlers when they put items in a specific order or nest things inside of each other.

This skill is exhibited by nineteen-month-old Arianna, who first lines up the painted tree cookies in a row on top of the light table and later lines up spoons side by side. Nesting-type loose parts in particular, such as bowls and boxes, assist young children in developing an understanding of seriation. Leonardo, sixteen months old, dumps three bowls upside down and puts the smallest bowl inside the largest one. He then places the medium bowl on top, but it does not fit neatly inside the other two. After several attempts, he is successful in his efforts to nest all three bowls inside one another.

REPRESENTATION OF EXPERIENCES AND IDEAS

Representation of experiences and ideas involves the capacity to use one thing to symbolize and represent another. Nineteen-month-old Arianna takes jar lids off the shelf, places them in a bowl, and stirs the pieces with a spoon. She pretends to take a bite of the mixture. She is using the lids to symbolize and represent food. Ian, thirty-three months old, uses wooden squares to represent a train track. Because most loose parts are nondescript, such as a piece of wood, a child can have the object take on the form of whatever is imagined.

NUMBER CONCEPTS

Number concepts develop as young children fill and dump objects. As thirty-month-old Nariah fills an empty bag with silk scarves, she notices the difference between empty and full. When she carries a crocheted coaster in each hand, places a spoon inside a bowl, or alternates her steps as she walks on stepping-stones, she begins to grasp an understanding of one-to-one correspondence. Nariah experiences the concept of "a lot" as she stacks multiple felt rings on the dowel of a paper towel holder and "not enough" when there is not one more crate to construct her house. She builds an understanding of numbers as she picks up each of four leaves and drops them into a basket.

SPATIAL RELATIONS

Understanding spatial relations is the cognitive ability to understand and interpret connections about how objects relate to each other. Young children's spatial learning is extended as they manipulate loose parts to build understanding of (1) objects in relation to other objects—putting seashells on the light table or in a box; (2) between oneself and other objects—"The ball went behind me"; and (3) between oneself and other people—"I am stacking tiles beside Mathew." Fitting loose parts into an opening, such as a wooden peg into a hole of a metal tin; connecting objects such as a nut and bolt; nesting measuring cups; and balancing tree cookies are all examples of how an understanding of spatial relations develops.

Language and Communication Learning and Development

Language has many uses as young children engage with loose parts. Sound effects may be used to describe actions, as evidenced by Samuel, who makes a "vrooming" sound while pretending that a piece of bark is a car, and later makes a whistling sound as he pretends that the bark is a train. The value of a loose part is that Samuel is able to change sound effects to match what his imagination has decided the bark to be. During play with loose parts, a child may use language to provide verbal instructions: "Stay there. Don't fall." Children may sing as they mix a concoction. A toddler often offers a running commentary when she explores loose parts in her hands, as Addy did when pretending to make muffins with dirt and water.

VOCABULARY

Play spaces thoughtfully filled with intriguing loose parts offer opportunities for infants and toddlers to actively practice new words. Vocabulary increases sharply as young children learn words to describe play objects and their characteristics, such as color, shape, size, texture, and weight. For instance, Saige uses the word "hebby" (heavy) to describe the rock she picks up, and Nariah says "soft" to describe a flannel piece of fabric. Teachers can support vocabulary development by using assorted adjectives, such as "rough" bark or "smooth, hard" tiles to describe the rich variations of loose parts.

ENCOURAGING COMMUNICATION

Loose parts invite infants and toddlers to explore properties of objects and verbally express their discoveries and creations. Because loose parts have unlimited play possibilities, teachers must closely observe actions and carefully listen to children's words while they play. For example, when a child plays with a cardboard tube, she has different ways to be creative and expressive with the object, and her words may reveal that the tube is a tunnel, tree, or home. When infants and toddlers are actively engaged with loose parts, an adult's role in supporting language development is to extend and expand their language and support their increased ability to communicate ideas by asking open-ended questions and using descriptive language.

Young children use language to communicate their needs and to direct others. Language can have a cognitive function, which involves naming, describing, or commenting about objects. As children explore loose parts, they use expressive language to name and describe objects. Leonardo says "rock hard," and Arianna, who wraps up a wooden clothespin with a small piece of burlap, says "baby." Luis uses the expression "Uh-oh" when his tower of tree blocks falls over. Language can also have an instrumental function, which includes asking, rejecting, and voicing desires. Matthew says "more" as he requests more crates for his structure, and Adam says "me throw" as he expresses his desire to throw a felted ball off the play loft.

Intentionality

Adding loose parts into an early learning environment is much more than simply placing a container or two of open-ended materials in an area. A basket of driftwood placed on the floor in a construction space may result in children simply dumping the wood on the floor. Children may ignore paper tubes left on a shelf or throw metal spoons. Such behaviors are not a reason to eliminate the loose parts from the environment, but rather an opportunity to carefully investigate children's intent, the type of materials provided, as well as where and how the loose parts are presented.

Children's Intent: Schema Learning

The infusion of loose parts involves intentionality, a thoughtful approach that incorporates a reflective cycle of observation, contemplation about challenges and possibilities, decision making, and action. The reflective process begins with careful observation of children to determine their interests or repeated patterns of behavior called *schemas*. "More specifically, a schema is a thread of thought which is demonstrated by repeated actions and patterns in children's play or art" (van Wijk 2008, 1). Young children learn and form cognitive structures in their minds through schema learning. Schema learning is a theory about how children learn and think. As children repeat an action such as throwing (trajectory schema), they develop a theory about how objects move in space. Characteristics of children engaged in schema play include intense concentration, persistence, complete absorption, a sense of wonder, and deep enjoyment and satisfaction.

Meade and Cubey assert that when children are investigating schemas, they are developing intellectual learning, which is an understanding of abstract concepts, ideas, and patterns, rather than academic learning, which is concerned with topic or specific content knowledge (2008). Once adults notice schemas, or patterns, in young children's play, they can respond in ways that extend and support children's learning.

Action schemas are one type of schema. Action schemas focus on ideas about movement in the physical world and are typically easy to identify, so it's a good way to begin schema recognition. Showing a fascination with throwing things, carrying objects around, knocking down a tower, and pouring water down a gutter are all examples of action schemas. "Repeating action schemas helps children to develop systematic ideas about the world and how it works" (van Wijk 2008, 6). When Rebecca, thirty-two months old, routinely pours water and watches the water flow, she is exhibiting a trajectory schema.

Diego repeatedly scoops sand into a bucket and then dumps it out, showing a filling and dumping schema. Julian demonstrates a grasping schema as he holds on to knotted cloth napkins. A transporting schema can be seen in Arianna when she fills her bag with silk scarves. Bryce likes to take things apart, showing a disconnecting schema. In each case the child has an intensity, an innate drive while exploring thought and concepts.

Below is a list of action schemas seen in infants' and toddlers' play. The schematic actions were identified by Susan Harper in her article "Schemas in Areas of Play" in the spring 2004 issue of *Playcentre Journal*.

Transporting—Picking things up, moving them, and putting them down or dumping them. Perhaps using a pram, bag, basket, truck or wheelbarrow. Usually has full hands.

Transforming—Materials that change shape, colour, consistency. Nothing stays clean.

Trajectory—Horizontal, vertical and diagonal movement of things and of self. Things fly through the air, child moves at a run.

Rotation and Circularity—Things that turn, loves wheels and/or balls. Exploring curved lines, loves circles.

Enclosing and Enveloping—Surrounds
things. Likes getting inside a
defined area, e.g. a block building,
tyre or barrel. Gets into boxes.
Covers completely, wraps up.
Hides. Gets into boxes and closes
lids.

Connecting—Joining things together.
Ties things up.

Disconnecting—Opposite: Takes things to pieces and/or scatters the parts.
(quoted in Meade and Cubey 2008, 27–29; and van Wijk 2008, 118–19)

Considerations for Presenting Loose Parts

Loose parts are fundamental materials in learning environments. When they are
intentionally placed in early childhood classrooms, the result is intriguing, challenging, and imaginative play possibilities for young children. Use the guidelines
below for designing provocations, and then once the loose parts are in place, wait
expectantly to observe how infants and toddlers respond to them.

Types and Presentation of Loose Parts to Provide

Loose parts should not be placed randomly in an environment, but with a
responsive, thoughtful, and intentional approach to support young children's
schema learning. Exploration with open-ended loose parts provides opportunity
to expand action schema learning, such as transporting, trajectory, transforming,
and connecting. When a teacher recognizes a schema, she can offer loose parts to
support and extend schema learning in the classroom as well as provide assistance to cope with children's frustrations that can happen.

For example, teachers Sara and Stacy observe Yoli's fascination with placing
materials inside other items. Recognizing an insertion schema, they add a let-
ter sorter with compartments into the learning environment along with a variety
of postcards and bookmarks as loose parts for Yoli to insert into the tray. Sharla
offers Julian multiple loose parts for grasping, including wooden spools, silicone
spatulas, and crocheted balls to encourage his grasping schema. When Janna
notes that Adam repetitively throws items inside the classroom, she acknowl-
edges his trajectory schema, and rather than reprimanding him for his behavior,

she supports his interest by placing loose parts in the form of soft balls and rings on the play loft platform. Upon Adam's morning arrival, he walks by the play loft, stops, glances at the platform, smiles, and swiftly climbs up the loft steps. He begins to enthusiastically throw balls off the loft. Janna responds in a way that promotes Adam's drive to throw objects, without hurting others.

Provocations

Loose parts are often presented to young children as provocations—invitations for play, curiosity, wonder, engagement, and discovery. They are materials simply and intentionally arranged for children to explore. Once the provocation is set up, teachers wait and observe how the children respond to them. Here are some ways to create provocations with loose parts that will support infants' and toddlers' learning and exploration.

Remember the following when setting up a loose parts provocation:

- Include open-ended items so that children can transform and transport them as they play.
- Incorporate interesting materials that children can use to design, construct, or make into props, such as natural, found objects like seashells, stones, tiles, ribbons, and fabric.
- Avoid placing glue or tape near loose parts. Once teachers or children adhere materials to themselves or something else, they are no longer loose parts.

SENSORY APPEAL

Children use their senses to explore and learn about their world. When loose parts appeal to infants' and toddlers' senses, children are more likely to spend time exploring and playing with them. Here are some ways to create provocations that appeal to children's senses:

- Organize loose parts by color, shape, texture, pattern, or design. For example, offer multicolor bottle caps, provide a collection of items shaped like circles, or include natural elements such as driftwood, seashells, and sea glass.

- Reflect on the aesthetic value of loose parts by thinking about found objects. Loose parts can be recycled or repurposed items, such as a case of thread spools or napkin rings.
- To increase interest, present items in odd numbers. A group of three or five containers is visually stronger than a group of two or four.

FUNCTION

The way loose parts are displayed in the environment can affect the way young children engage with them. When setting up the space, consider what will happen there. Will the materials be used to build, engage in imaginative play, or encourage sensory exploration?

Keep the following in mind when considering the function of your provocation:

- Think about the containers that will hold the loose parts and how they will fit in the work space. The way teachers present loose parts can promote independent or collaborative interactions.
- Try arranging the same materials in a variety of spaces to expand possibilities and interest during play. Young children play differently indoors, outdoors, and on a tabletop or floor.
- Keep materials out for several days so infants and toddlers have time to become familiar with them. Play becomes more complex when children have the opportunity to tinker with the items.
- Include an element of surprise every now and again that is attractive and unexpected. For example, a framed piece of fabric or a mirror as a work surface.

ACCESSIBILITY

When arranging loose parts, think about how infants and toddlers will access them. Set up loose parts so children can see and reach objects. Making sure parts are accessible also involves finding the right position for materials in the play space and allowing time for exploration. To make loose parts more accessible, consider the following:

- Place items on low shelves or in open baskets and containers within children's reach. For infants this involves placement of objects on the floor.

- Arrange smaller items in front of taller ones so children can see what is available.
- Allow ample time for children to explore materials and offer them opportunities to move items around the work space.
- Organize items in baskets, compartment containers, and shelving units to keep the work space ordered, clutter free, and clean. This helps children find items that they are looking for easily, reducing conflicts.

QUANTITY

It's hard to find the right number of loose parts to display at a time. Too many items can be overwhelming and overstimulating for young children. Too few materials can frustrate children and limit their opportunities for play. This may cause conflicts among children trying to work with limited resources. Here is a tip for finding the right balance when deciding how many objects to include in a provocation:

- One or two items are not enough to allow for rich explorations. Offering more items allows for more complex play. For example, a provocation with large quantities of driftwood is stronger than a provocation with only a few pieces of driftwood placed among seashells, stones, and sea glass.

SPACE

Space can be a valuable tool in a provocation. Space can be the work space where a child manipulates materials, such as a tabletop or mat, or space can be the area between items in a display. Infants and toddlers need enough space to actively engage with loose parts. To use space in a provocation, try the following:

- Define the space using lambskin rugs, trays, mats, picture frames, tabletops, area rugs, or pieces of fabric.
- Allow enough space for children to work.
- Avoid overwhelming the area with too many objects or containers.
- Maintain a focal point at children's eye level to retain children's interest.
- Play with the height of materials by placing a basket on an overturned container or base.
- Consider hiding a bucket or box under fabric to create height.
- Place loose parts on top of a nonbreakable mirror to create dimension.

TEXTURE

Many young children learn about their world through their sense of touch. Provide infants and toddlers with a variety of textures to help them learn. Loose parts' textures give them depth, warmth, softness, roughness, and sometimes an emotional component. It also adds dimension to a provocation and appeals to children's senses, both tactilely and visually. Here are some ways to incorporate texture into the environment:

- Layer different textures to add depth. Natural loose parts, for instance, can include stones that are smooth and hard, prickly pinecones, and rough bark.
- Add a background fabric, like rough burlap, a silky scarf, or rich velvet.

COLOR

Color consists of three primary attributes: *hue* (the name of the color), *value* (how dark or light it is), and *intensity* (how dull or bright it is). When displaying loose parts, displaying materials by color can make a provocation seem more organized, harmonious, and distinct:

- Choose a color palette with shades that complement each other and work together to create harmony and interest.
- Contrasting colors create emphasis. For example, a purple fabric under yellow loose parts or a green place mat with red leaves on top will offer a dramatic visual effect.

TRANSPARENCY AND LIGHT

Young children are fascinated with light, color, and shadows. Light and transparency provide depth to the provocation and attract young children's attention. Here are some ways to incorporate light, color, and transparency:

- Collect colorful, transparent items such as glass stones, jewels, and acrylic or plastic containers.
- Arrange materials in clear plastic jars and containers so their vibrant colors stand out.
- For visual impact, provide interesting backgrounds to the work space, such as nonbreakable mirrors, light tables, or black fabric.

Transforming Early Learning Environments

As authors, our journey over the past two years has transformed our thinking about loose parts. We now view loose parts as an educational philosophy rather than just intriguing materials with play potential. To embrace loose parts as an educational philosophy, teachers need mentoring and coaching from an experienced early childhood educator who works alongside them to provide guidance about loose parts principles, exchange information about loose parts in a classroom setting, identify children's interests/ideas/theories in their play with loose parts, and reflect on experiences and next steps for learning. Teachers must practice in order to truly grasp the rich nature of the reflective process (noticing, recognizing, reflecting, and decision making), view children as capable and competent, and support their learning.

During the writing and photographing of this book, we had the pleasure of working with several exceptional teachers who were intrigued with loose parts. Our role evolved from authors to mentors and collaborators in transforming early learning environments. Provocative discussions with these teachers revealed several fundamental changes to their views once loose parts were incorporated into the learning environment:

Teachers' understanding of loose parts expanded to include wide varieties of materials for infants and toddlers. Initially, the infant and toddler environments included only soft materials because they were safe. Now teachers see the benefit of incorporating materials with different properties to support children's extended learning.

Teachers' vision of loose parts increased to realize that they can be incorporated throughout the entire classroom, not just in a specific area. Originally, only the block area contained loose parts, but gradually they expanded to all areas of the classroom, which positively impacted how young children played in each play space.

Teachers' comfort with incorporating loose parts into their learning environment increased. One teacher reported how the children's play in her classroom became more imaginative and complex when they were allowed to move materials throughout the classroom. She realized she had wanted to keep materials in designated areas and that she was constantly telling children *no*. But when she relinquished her control, resistance diminished and children engaged in richer play.

Teachers recognized the importance of how loose parts are selected. They reported seeing how intentionally choosing materials based on children's interests and inquiries supported their curriculum planning. They were better able to identify children's skills, plan meaningful curriculum, and articulate children's learning. Schema recognition became a regular occurrence, followed by the identification of loose parts to promote children's schema learning.

Teachers emphasized the significance of how loose parts are displayed for young children. Considerations for presenting materials, such as types, accessibility, quantity, and aesthetics, were elements the teachers had not contemplated in the past. They reported that the way materials were presented changed how infants and toddlers approached and interacted with the loose parts.

Teachers learned that loose parts should be left in the environment for children to access independently and use during one-on-one play.

Teachers discovered the importance of time. First, it takes time for young children to adjust to loose parts play when they are used to commercial toys. Second, it is important to allow infants and toddlers ample time to explore loose parts.

Teachers learned to leave materials in the environment so that children become familiar with their properties and have time to try different possibilities.

Teachers gleaned that it is important to keep certain play objects in the environment while supplementing those objects with loose parts. Dolls, for example, support the development of caring and nurturing skills and help young children work through strong emotions. Loose parts such as blankets, scarves, and fabric allow children an opportunity to wrap baby dolls in a caring way. Other loose parts, such as a piece of wood or large glass stones, can be used symbolically as bottles or food for feeding babies.

Types of Play with Loose Parts

The chapters that follow are organized according to specific play characteristics that are visible in young children's play, such as dumping, inserting, disconnecting, and pushing/pulling. This organizational method was chosen to illustrate how infants and toddlers may use loose parts. The following three parts—object, assembly, and instrumental explorations—are play actions described in 1970 by Sinclair (Casby 2003a). Object exploration consists of investigating objects through the senses, such as touching, shaking, and mouthing. Assembly exploration involves the process of combining objects in play, such as stacking rocks, and instrumental exploration is characterized as using one object to act upon another, such as using a spoon to bang a metal lid. Part 5, "Locomotion," reveals how loose parts support infants' and toddlers' development and learning as they become mobile and master balancing, transporting, climbing, and swinging. In part 6, action comprises trajectory, transporting, pretending, and constructing.

It's important to note that though we categorize types of play actions, loose parts are rarely used for a single purpose in the classroom. That is, a child may use the same loose part—a tile, for example—in many different ways, such as for stacking, constructing, pretending, filling/dumping, and transporting.

This was the case with Adam. We set up gray plastic yarn spindles and cardboard rings outdoors to illustrate how loose parts can be used for throwing. The spindles were placed in a row, one on top of each stepping stone, and the rings set in a bowl nearby.

The idea was for the older toddlers to throw the rings over the yarn spindles, as in the game of ring toss. As we waited expectantly for the children to join us, Adam came outdoors and promptly kicked over each standing spindle in succession. He carefully stood each spindle back up and proceeded to jump over each one. Next, he took a pitcher, filled it with water from the water table, and poured water down the open center of a spindle. Never was a ring tossed around a spindle. This shows the powerful nature of loose parts as they possess infinite play possibilities. As you view each chapter, consider the potential of each loose part beyond the chapter's theme and imagine how a young child might use it.

Conclusion

We hope you are inspired by the ideas and images in this book and are encouraged to add loose parts that provoke exploration into infant/toddler learning environments in an intentional, responsive, and aesthetically pleasing way. Once the loose parts are in place, stand back and watch as children engage with the materials in powerful and amazing ways. Be prepared to be surprised and delighted.

Part 2
Object Exploration

Hearing

Looking

Touching

Grasping

When we treat children's play as seriously as it deserves, we are helping them feel the joy that's to be found in the creative spirit. We're helping ourselves stay in touch with that spirit too. It's the things we play with and the people who help us play that make a great difference in our lives.

—FRED ROGERS
THE WORLD ACCORDING TO MISTER ROGERS: IMPORTANT THINGS TO REMEMBER

Every moment infants and toddlers are awake, they are engaged in exploration. They move their arms toward a nearby object, or they track an item that is moving within their eyesight. In other words, they are active explorers of their environment. This idea is not new. Piaget (1952) stressed that children under age two use their senses and motor skills to gain information about the world around them. Intelligence takes the form of action and originates from an infant's busy transaction with objects in the environment. The child's job is to figure out how things work.

When infants and toddlers are manipulating, mouthing, listening, and looking at loose parts, they discover properties and possibilities for action that different objects offer. During active exploration of loose parts, infants and toddlers are gaining perceptual-motor skills, or the ability to successfully obtain information through the senses, understand it, and react appropriately. A bamboo cup and a variety of silicone-covered spatulas and spoons provide ten-month-old Micco with multiple exploration opportunities to gain both of these skills and abilities. The spoons are safe and flexibly coated so that he can mouth them, turn them, and bring them close to his eyes. At the same time, he is using all of his senses to explore the loose parts, thus increasing the development of his sensory systems.

During their first year of life, infants develop a series of actions that they apply to a variety of objects. In the process, they learn to adjust their movements based on the specific characteristics of that particular object. For instance, they tighten their grip on an object with a soft surface but apply less pressure when the surface is rough. As infants become more experienced with the manipulation of different types of loose parts, they begin to spend more time observing, examining, and moving them and spend less time orally inspecting them.

Jacob is beginning to crawl and move around and is attracted to loose parts that roll. To support his interest, the teachers place an attractive container of o-balls (balls with finger holes) and pinecones he can easily grasp. Jacob spends part of the day exploring the contents of the container and making them roll down a small ramp. As young children develop an intimate understanding of how an object works, their play is less magical and becomes more complex and effective. This allows them to plan, scheme, and begin to use objects as tools (Gopnik, Meltzoff, and Kuhl 1999).

Considering the exploratory nature of infants and toddlers, adults need to offer them opportunities to interact with loose parts that can be manipulated in a variety of ways. In contrast with wind-up mobiles or electric toys, which are passive and train young children to immediately be amused and entertained, loose parts are activated when infants and toddlers play with them, and children learn to entertain themselves. In other words, loose parts offer the best choice for active exploration because the infants and toddlers are actively engaged in and in charge of their own play. Balls of different sizes and textures allow Josiah to throw and retrieve them as he visually tracks them. Scarves and soft blankets engage Ariana in active play as she envelops and soothes herself with them. The best objects and materials for infants and toddlers to explore do not need to be fancy; they just need to be thoughtfully selected. The best loose parts are those that allow young children to be as active and competent as possible.

CHAPTER 2
Looking

Infants learn to see over a period of time. They learn to accurately move their gaze and to focus. They also learn to use and process the information their eyes send to their brain. This is an important part of cognitive development. Vision, and how the brain uses visual information, is a learned skill, similar to walking and talking.

From birth, infants explore the wonder of the world with their eyes. Even before they learn to reach and grab objects or crawl and sit up, their eyes are providing them with important knowledge about their world. As children grow and actively engage with their environment in more systematic and intentional ways, their distance vision, or the ability to see objects twenty feet away, begins to mature.

Julian, nine months old, tracks an LED light as the teacher moves it. Not only can he now track objects with efficient eye movement, but he can also successfully reach and grasp them. Contrasting and bright colors as well as complex patterns continue to appeal to Julian at this age. Over time, young children begin to differentiate among objects as evidenced by their ability to classify loose parts.

When adults place different loose parts near an infant's reach, they are supporting important visual stimulation and information. Loose parts can support infants' development of visual acuity (the clarity or sharpness of vision). They can also help increase their ability to focus. When Jesenia, nine months old, focuses on a black-and-white napkin or colorful pom-poms, she is exercising the ciliary muscles inside her eyes. As she focuses her eyes, these muscles automatically contract or relax the shape of the eye's lens. This projects a clear image onto the receiving surface, or retina, at the back of the eye. This is similar to adjusting the lens of a camera to get a perfectly focused photograph.

Making Rainbows

On a warm, sunny day, Sharla, the teacher, decides to place bottles filled with colorful water on the windowsill. The sunlight passes through the colored water, casting a beautiful rainbow on the floor. Ten-month-old Micco, who is on his tummy, reaches for the rainbow and watches as the light reflects off his hand. As Micco rolls over onto his back, Sharla brings one of the bottles down and places it next to him. He first explores the bottle with his mouth and starts lifting it off and placing it back on his tummy. As the bottle moves, the sunlight from the window passes through it and the colored light reflects off the wall near him. He stops his movements and focuses intently as he watches the light spots on the wall. Sharla watches in fascination as Micco kicks his feet in excitement every time the light spot moves.

The exploration of the bottles continues as Sharla moves them to the light table and then to an overhead projector for the toddlers in the group to explore. The toddlers notice how the light reflects off the walls, and then they realize that it is also reflecting off their bodies. Laughter permeates the room, and the toddlers begin to make important connections to how light reflects off different surfaces.

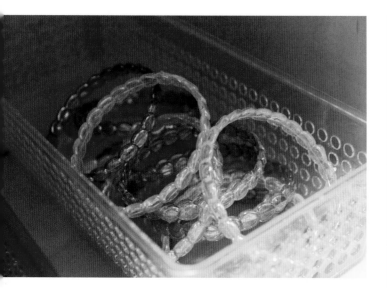

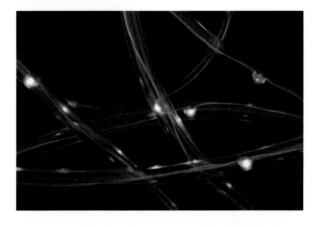

Julian first investigates the fickering LED candles with fascination and then he entangles himself in the LED rope as Sharla engages him in an exploration of light.

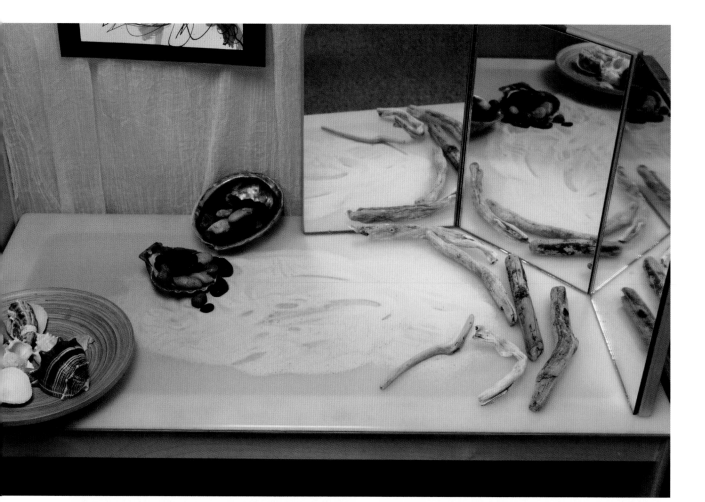

An arrangement of sand, driftwood, and rocks on the light table presents a visually appealing provocation of natural elements for the children to explore.

CHAPTER 3
Touching

Touch is the most fundamental means of contact with the world. Infants spend most of their waking hours touching their mouths and the rest of their bodies. This is, in part, an organized exploratory behavior. Since our skin is one of the most sensitive parts of our body and provides much information about the world and its messages, it makes sense that young children spend so much time exploring how touch feels to their bodies.

As infants and toddlers reach to touch different objects, they begin to distinguish what gives them pleasure and what may cause pain. They begin to discover what they like and dislike. Loose parts offer children multiple opportunities to explore surfaces. Nine-month-old Jesenia explores embroidery hoops holding silky fabric, soft blankets, and smooth or rippled wood pieces. She engages in different types of exploration. She discovers that satin can feel comfortable on her skin, while pieces of wool feel raspy and uncomfortable. Providing different objects to touch and compare—crocheted coasters made with different types of yarn, a variety of balls made from different materials, a wooden spoon and a metal one—helps infants and toddlers differentiate textures and begin to test what they prefer.

The Leathery Palm

Rich brown leaf stalks from a friend's giant palm tree regularly shed onto the ground of Lisa's backyard. Intrigued by the properties of these stalks, she asks her friend if she can have some. She wonders if the children in her classroom will find them as captivating as she does. Lately Lisa has noticed the children's deep interest in texture and how they repeatedly touch materials displayed in the texture frames—hard, scratchy twigs; corrugated copper; bumpy fabric; and soft cork. They are also fascinated with sand, water, and clay explorations. From observing the children's actions, she gets a sense of their intention to compare surfaces and supports their interest in texture by gathering the palm stalks and bringing them to the classroom for children to explore. Lisa places the broad wedge-shaped leaf stalks into a pile near the sand area along with a basket of leathery bark. The stalks are cut into various lengths, which reveal the fibrous interior of the exposed edges. Rebecca, thirty-two months old, is the first child to approach the pile. She grasps a palm

stalk at its base and rubs her hand across the thick, leathery brown exterior. Back and forth her hand slides on the tough, smooth surface. Her focus then shifts to the end of the palm stalk, which consists of soft compacted fibers of the leaf stalk. Rebecca is attentive as she touches the open edge. Perhaps she expects the surface to be stiff like the outside shell rather than soft. She strokes the silky, feathery tissue in upward motions and then strokes the firm exterior again. On a second occasion, she reaches into the wicker basket and pulls out the tough bark. She gently rubs the hard, leathery surface with her hand and then investigates the bark by stroking it with her bare foot. Each tactile experience with the palm tree sections gives Rebecca more and more information about her natural world.

Mathew strokes the varying fabric textures that were placed into the embroidery hoops for children to explore their sense of touch.

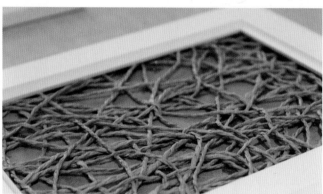

Ian actively explores a variety of texture frames mounted on the wall. He rubs his hand on small tree cookies, pats them, and listens to see if a sound is produced. Another frame containing thin tree branches captures his attention. He runs his fingers up and down the sticks, feeling their rough, hard texture.

CHAPTER 4

Hearing

Sound inherently supports infants' and toddlers' cognitive development. Loose parts that produce sound offer young children an opportunity to figure out how objects work in connection with their actions. For example, when infants or toddlers shake a small gourd rattle, they gain understanding of how their actions influence the world they inhabit. This cause-and-effect knowledge increases their self-awareness and ability to control their environment. Sound encourages children to explore loose parts. They learn to localize sound and respond to the sound with interest. They tend to follow and be interested in objects that move while producing sound.

A bouncing ball with a jingle bell inside captures their attention. The visible and audible properties of the ball correspond to a single, unitary event. The rate at which the jingle bell sounds correlates directly with the rolling of the ball. As young children's memory increases, they will remember the cause of the reaction. They will discover that some things make noise when shaken or banged, and they will experiment with different ways to make it happen again. When infants and toddlers interact with loose parts that produce sound, they begin to connect when two perceptual modes (sound and sight) pertain to one object or event. When Lonzo, twenty-one months old, takes a metal spoon and bangs on a metal lid, imitating Bryce who is doing the same action, he will have recognized the sound and replicated it on his own. Eventually Lonzo will identify that objects produce various sounds when manipulated, and he will be able to associate sounds with specific objects. For example, he will learn that the sound of a pot being banged with a metal spoon is different than the sound of the same pot being banged with a wooden spoon. As young children recognize different sounds, they are also developing a sense of the space between the object and their own position in that space—in other words, sound localization.

Making Sounds in the Kitchen

The older toddlers have been showing an interest in sound and music. Sara and Stacey, the classroom teachers, intentionally place a series of metal containers and kitchen utensils in the learning environment to engage the children in sound making. The moment Ian and Ethan enter the classroom, they are drawn to this new provocation. They immediately start testing the different utensils by banging and running spoons up and down the ridged bread tubes and muffin tins. They laugh and encourage each other to make louder sounds. Nariah comes over and starts taking the spoons and containers into the kitchen area, stating, "In kitchen." The boys come over and take the spoons and trays and continue making sounds. Nariah pretends that she is making soup by using a stirring motion with one of the spoons. She then proceeds to match a spoon to each container. She looks over to where the boys are still making sounds, and she slowly begins to imitate them. This moment shows that loose parts can support every child's interests and ideas. Loose parts do not belong in just one space; they can be moved as children engage with them differently. In the end, Nariah returns the utensils to the original music space, where she continues to enjoy them.

Micco delights in the sound of dry
seeds rattling inside the gourd.

A simple zigzag paper towel holder offers toddlers hours of entertainment. Adam and Nariah enjoy listening to the clinking sound of metal napkin rings sliding down the metal zigzag dowel.

CHAPTER 5

Grasping

The ability to grasp objects begins at birth. As infants' ability to grasp and release objects becomes more intentional, a new world of possibilities is within their reach. Their play becomes more complex; they begin to feed themselves and grasp the edges of furniture to cruise around the room. Their exploration of objects becomes more sophisticated as they intentionally reach to grasp a maple wooden ring with colorful

ribbons attached that visually catches their attention. Knots tied in the middle of black-and-white napkins in a basket make it easy for the infants to grasp them.

The process of *prehension* (the action of grasping) begins with the *grasp reflex*, the reaction when the infant's palm is stroked gently. Initially, infants pick up objects using a *palmar grasp*, in which an object is secured in the center of their palm without the use of their thumb. As infants acquire more control over the movement of their hands, they use a *raking grasp* by spreading out their fingers and pulling an object into the palm of the hand. Eventually infants develop the ability to grasp an object using their thumb and index finger in a *pincer grasp*. But in order for infants to use their hands efficiently they need to have a strong and stable core. They must be able to maintain a steady position with their trunk and neck muscles, as well as stabilize their shoulders to allow their hands to move freely. Placing small crocheted pillows, wooden rings, and thick pull ropes in front of infants as they lie on their stomach encourages them to reach and develop their core muscles. During the second year of life, toddlers' small-motor skills improve and they are able to hold both large and small objects with more proficiency. Increased fine-motor skills help toddlers use their fingers and thumbs independently and perform more complex small-motor skills, such as sorting loose parts, picking up loose parts with a spoon, and turning a jar lid.

Micco Discovers Loose Parts

There is nothing more exciting than watching an infant discover his hands for the first time. From the moment Micco finds his hands, he spends time moving them in front of his eyes. Teacher Sharla watches in fascination every day as he becomes more adept at moving his hands and slowly begins to use them more effectively. To support his development, she places a variety of soft, colorful silicone cups and rings with ribbons attached on the floor. Sharla watches as Micco begins to reach for them. He is focused and shows an apparent determination to grasp them. His excitement can be measured by the way he moves his feet each time he touches one of the cups. After a few weeks, he begins to grasp and hold a wooden ring with colorful ribbons attached. As he gains in his grasping skill, Micco starts grasping and holding o-balls and dropping them to see what happens. He smiles as he watches them fall.

Jesenia firmly grasps the dog pull rope. The rope's loop and knot make it easier for her to hold.

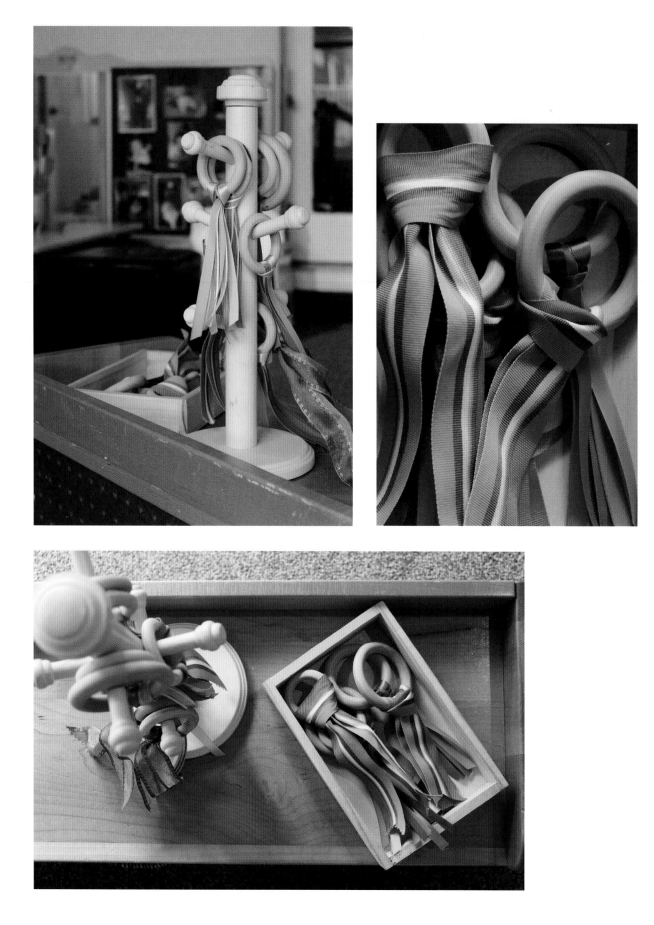

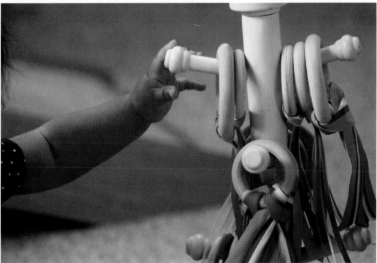

The infants find silicone kitchen utensils particularly easy to grasp.

Part 3
Assembly
Exploration

Belonging for young children is a place where they feel comfortable enough to play without having to look over their shoulders seeking approval or dodging disapproval, to explore without fear, to redefine their space, and to use materials to create a personal sense of order, patterns, and structure.

—BEV BOS AND ROSEVILLE COMMUNITY PRESCHOOL STAFF

Filling and Dumping

Connecting and Disconnecting

Stacking

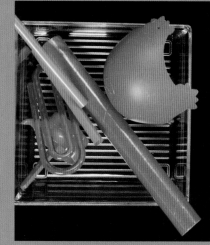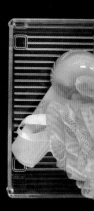

Sorting and Classifying

Infants and toddlers come equipped with an innate curiosity about their environment. As their development progresses, they move from object exploration to assembly exploration, which includes a fascination with stacking, nesting, filling, dumping, and inserting. Children want to know how things fit together and how things are similar or different. Through active assembly, infants and toddlers acquire important information about how specific objects work. They demonstrate how to manipulate and combine loose parts. They sort and classify objects in different configurations. At first the combinations may seem to be random and not based on defined spatial, categorical, or functional properties of an object. As young children's understanding deepens, they assemble loose parts in more complex ways, as demonstrated in their ability to classify. Ian, thirty-three months old, looks at the red, white, and black wooden circles in opposite-colored containers. He immediately says, "No. Not okay." He walks over to the shelf, dumps all the circles on the floor, and rearranges them. He places black circles in the black container, white in the white container, and red in the red. He has made a mental classification and proceeds to move the circles until he is satisfied.

Assembly is a complex system of play that engages a deep knowledge and understanding of object coherence, relevance, and solidity that develops over time as infants and toddlers explore loose parts. As young children play with familiar objects found in the environment, they view objects from different points of view. Thus begins the understanding of the three-dimensional (3-D) form.

By the time they are a year old, infants methodically change how they manipulate objects. For instance, they will take a set of blocks and

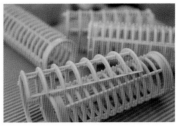

explore different possibilities of assembly. They will place the blocks in different combinations while carefully observing their positions. This eventually leads them to build a stable tower and then knock it down with the same level of pleasure (Gopnik 2009). Sixteen-month-old Leonardo finds a metal paper towel holder with a variety of bracelets, round scrunchies, and felted circles stacked on it. He takes them off and starts to stack them one on top of another. When they topple over, he starts placing them back on the holder.

As children enter late infancy (twelve months), they scientifically explore objects to recognize attributes. They assemble or sort and classify loose parts by lining up or separating them based on color, number, object identity, or shape. They compare and contrast specific attributes of each object: "Leaves go together, but the yellow leaves go with the yellow buttons." This type of exploration presents multiple possibilities and challenges that stimulate their thinking.

Unlike puzzles, loose parts offer toddlers multiple opportunities to solve problems and find different solutions to a challenge. When Ethan takes a muffin tin and sorts large pebbles by color, he is comparing and contrasting differences and similarities. This type of classification experience can be used in the future to solve more complex scientific and mathematical equations. As toddlers begin to recognize common attributes and differences of objects, they also begin to acquire the concept of identity—the ability to define oneself as a unique person with a sense of self. They make mental connections to patterns and discern differences and similarities.

CHAPTER 6
Stacking

Stacking boxes, wooden bowls, tree cookies, and other loose parts supports perceptual-motor development, creativity, and the acquisition of scientific and mathematical concepts. Perceptual-motor skills allow sensory information to be successfully obtained and understood with appropriate reaction. *Perception* refers to the process of obtaining information, and motor refers to the outcome of movement. Thus perceptual-motor activities require children to use their brain and body together to accomplish tasks. As Nariah, thirty months old, stacks wooden tree blocks together, she has to use her fine-motor skills, balance, and coordination. She has to carefully place one tree block on top of another, observing how she places it so that it is balanced and will not fall. She has to think the process through, which requires tremendous coordination of all her senses, cognition, and physical abilities.

Observe young children engaged in stacking and you will notice how they become more creative as they work on more complex stacking possibilities. Ian, thirty-three months old, is capable of combining several loose parts to represent train tracks that run through tall towers. He uses tiles, first lining them up on the floor for the track and then stacking the same tiles to build towers around the track. He is creative and attempts different stacking combinations before he is satisfied with his work. In the process of stacking loose parts, older infants and toddlers develop self-competence and delight in their achievements.

Stacking promotes the development of scientific thinking. At first young children will stack objects vertically, lay them down, and line them up. They often repeat the same stacking patterns and, once mastered, move on to more complex combinations. As their skills grow, they build taller towers and attempt to figure out what made the tower topple over. Diego, thirty-four months old, stacks three tiles on top of one another, stops, and observes the short tower. He then takes another tile and carefully places it on top. This time the tile is not perfectly centered and the tower topples over. He steps back and attempts to understand what happened. He starts another tower, and this time he can add up to ten tiles. The tower remains standing as he walks away. Diego is gaining an understanding of balance; tiles need to be placed perfectly centered for the structure to remain stable. As the tower topples over, he is exploring concepts of gravity and force.

Rock Stacking on the Wall

Eighteen-month-old Saige is an observant risk taker who spends her time moving from one new exploration to another, fully immersing herself in the process. She thrives in the

novelty of things, and it is common to see her manipulating and exploring new loose parts. She particularly enjoys the rocks strategically placed around the outdoor environment of Cheri's family early child care and education program. A good amount of her time is spent stacking the heavy gray rocks to create beautiful arrangements that expand the entire cinder block wall. Her concentration is impressive as she finds small nooks to carefully place rocks on top of one another. When she manages to stack three rocks, she laughs in delight. Saige often reorganizes the rocks placed on the wall by other children by either stacking them on different nooks or putting them in a basket and carrying the heavy load to a nearby shelf.

Cheri says that Saige loves to clean and organize, and as educators we think it is impressive to see Saige so skillfully handle the rocks. With determination and support, toddlers are capable of manipulating heavy rocks to create rock sculptures that represent their ideas and thinking.

Nicholas and Yoli delight in stacking manufactured tile samples high and then watching them fall.

Ian tests his abilities by stacking tree cookie rings on wooden dowels. He moves the rings around until he is satisfied that he has the same number of cookies on each dowel. His mathematical ability is rudimentary, yet he can visually approximate quantity.

CHAPTER 7
Filling and Dumping

Through filling and dumping, older infants and toddlers acquire important information that leads to an increase in cognition. They learn the concepts of "empty" and "full" and acquire a rudimentary understanding of quantity, space, trajectory, and cause and effect. They are fascinated with exploring how many and what types of items can fit in containers of all shapes and sizes. They enjoy the process of filling baskets and bags with different items they find in the environment. For instance, while sitting on the ground with a teacher, Samuel, thirty months old, explores a variety of containers filled with cocoa mulch. First, he tips a container of cocoa mulch and dumps all of it into the tub. Then he picks up a coconut shell, methodically fills it with cocoa mulch, and transfers the mulch into another container. Through these actions, Samuel begins to recognize how much it takes (quantity) to fill differently sized containers with more or less mulch. He acquires a deeper understanding of space as he investigates how cocoa mulch fills containers. He obtains further knowledge of spatial relationships—that is, the concept of where an object is in relation to another object, as he pours mulch from above, over his outstretched hand, or as he moves his body into different positions in space while playing with the cocoa mulch. Samuel is captivated with trajectory, or movement in space, as he dumps mulch from different heights. As he purposefully pours cocoa mulch onto various surfaces, he gains knowledge of cause and effect. When he pours mulch onto the slide, it cascades down. The cocoa mulch poured between the wooden slats of a platform disappears, while the cocoa mulch poured into wet grass becomes sticky. Samuel's engagement with filling and dumping cocoa mulch demonstrates how infants and toddlers build cognitive concepts and competence as they explore the physical properties of objects.

Jacob Transports

With energy and enthusiasm, twelve-month-old Jacob fills up any kind of a container with sand, water, birdseed, or gravel and then promptly empties the contents. This repetition of filling and dumping illustrates his passion for transporting, as he is completely absorbed with his actions. He exhibits a sense of wonder each time a substance tumbles out of the bucket, and then he quickly fills it once more, as if to confirm that the same result will happen. Jacob also delights in anything with wheels that he can push. Marlysa helps him fill the bed of a giant dump truck with pinecones. Off he goes, hands clutched to the truck's sides, as he races around the concrete path. He dumps out his load and heads back for another. The filling and dumping sequence continues until all of the pinecones have been transported to the sand area. On another occasion, Jacob discovers the wheelbarrow. Addy needs pipe fittings to serve as food in her restaurant, so Jacob loads

them into the wheelbarrow and begins to slowly move forward. The wheelbarrow tips to the side, and all the fittings spill out. Once again, he loads up the fittings. It takes some time for him to manage the balance required, but he persists until he masters control. Eventually he arrives at the restaurant and delivers the food by dumping it onto the ground.

Alvin spends time filling containers with colorful aquarium gravel. He transfers gravel from a small metal cup to a larger metal container, pausing and observing as the gravel empties into the larger bowl. He fills and dumps and fills again with apparent intentionality. He is beginning to understand the concept of quantity and space. Note: Always use aquarium gravel with careful adult supervision.

Yoli uses extra-large tempered glass stones to represent soap bubbles as she washes dishes and milk as she pretends to make a drink.

Marlysa and Makayla are intent on filling funnels with sand. Marlysa uses a spoon to help guide the sand into the funnel.

CHAPTER 8

Connecting and Disconnecting

Older infants and toddlers are often seen tying ribbons and rope around different objects. They enjoy sticking different colored tape on paper and wooden toys and then taking it off. Toddlers connect and disconnect giant paper clips, metal springs, and items with Velcro. Disconnect schema is also seen when older infants and toddlers take apart a wood structure or objects that they had tied together. Connect and disconnect schemas give us an insight into young children's thinking and understanding of the world in which they live. As they repeatedly connect and disconnect loose parts, children develop structures for thinking (van Wijk 2008). When Yoli, thirty-three months old, takes a large paper clip and connects it to another paper clip, she begins to recognize how items belong together. She then transfers the new knowledge to other explorations, such as when she connects and places caps on different jars to make them fit together.

Toddlers may stick three small tubes together to create a long tube that they can use as a ramp, or they may connect cove molding to a magnetic wall. This gives them the opportunity to wonder and ask, "What will happen if I place an item on the wall? Will it stick or fall?"

Nariah, thirty months old, discovers a new exploration consisting of spice cans with magnetic backs that attach to a metal broiler tray. Colorful pom-poms inside each can are visible through the clear acrylic lids. She looks at the cans, fascinated by the colors inside. Her attention shifts from looking at the colorful pom-pom designs to pulling the cans off the broiler tray. It takes a lot of her strength to pull the cans off. Two cans adhere to each other when she accidentally touches the can bottoms together. An interest in connecting and disconnecting begins.

As older infants and toddlers connect and disconnect loose parts, they move from an early, simplistic understanding of how things work into more complex thinking of what makes objects connect and disconnect. This type of schema increases cognitive development and promotes higher-level thinking and meaning making. The connect and disconnect schemas are also a precursor to reading and writing since they give young children the preparatory knowledge that letters connect into words, and later words connect into sentences to help them express their ideas.

How Do the Clothespins Work?

For the past week, Sharla and the infants have been exploring colorful boxes, thread spools, and clothespins contained inside transparent shaker bottles. Leonardo is especially interested in taking the clothespins out of the bottle. Responding to his curiosity, Sharla shows him how to open and close a clothespin by placing a finger on each prong and pushing the prongs down. Leonardo is developing his fine-motor skills and is always ready for a new challenge. He eagerly watches as Sharla places his fingers on each prong and helps him push them together. He attempts to make the peg open and finds that this is a difficult task. Observing his attempts, Sharla takes the clothespins and connects them around the top edge of a plastic bucket. She thinks that this will facilitate Leonardo's attempts to figure out how the mechanism works. Leonardo places the bucket between his legs and presses on the prongs, managing to disconnect the first clothespin from the bucket. He does the same with all the other clothespins clipped to the bucket's edge. This simple connecting and disconnecting activity has strengthened the bond between Leonardo and Sharla.

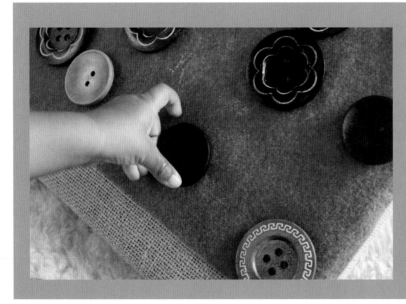

Leonardo uses his strength to pull the Velcro buttons off the felt.

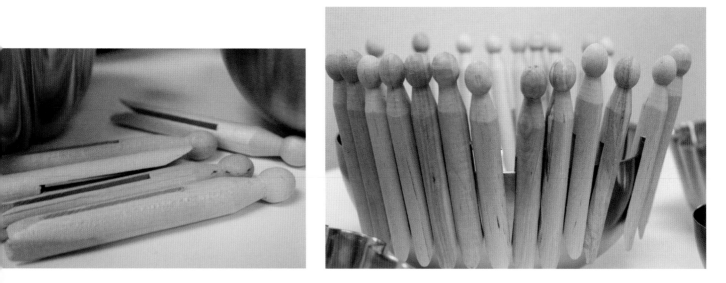

Nicholas spends a long time carefully placing the clothespins around the metal bowl until the rim is fully covered. He tests different ways to place the clothespins along the rippled edge of the bundt pan and finally manages to connect a couple of them on the mold.

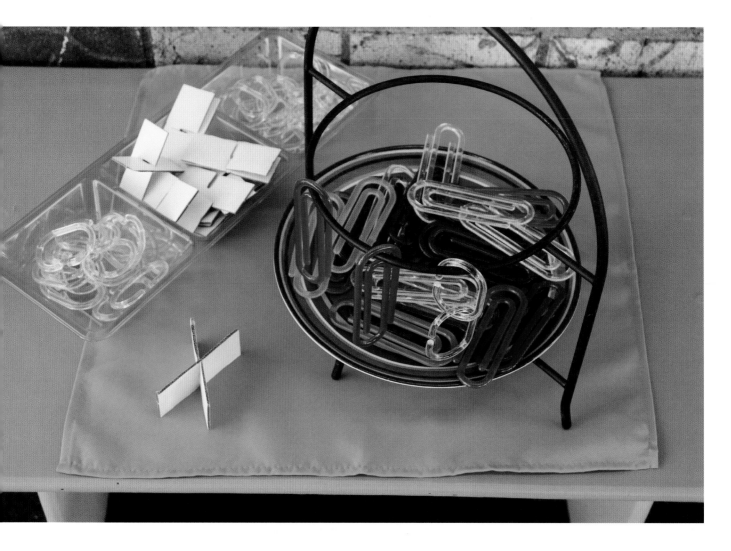

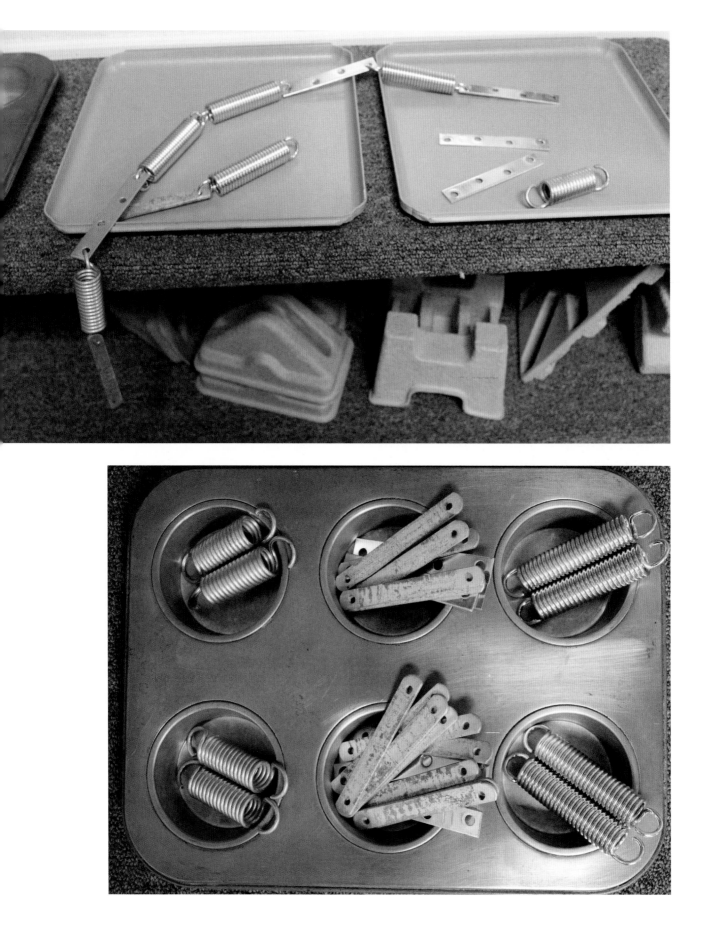

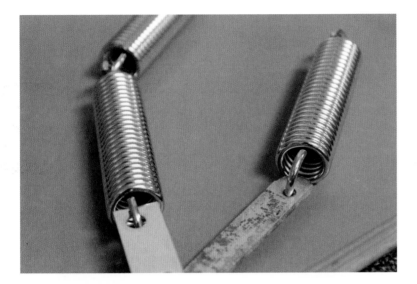

Yoli connects metal springs onto the bucket's edge, but the weight of the springs overturns the bucket. Yoli perseveres, and after multiple attempts she manages to connect all the springs without the bucket overturning. She claps and laughs as she says, "Did it!"

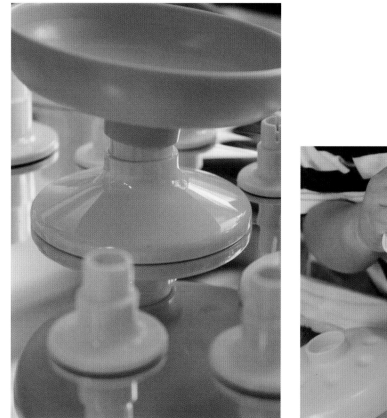

CHAPTER 9

Sorting and Classifying

Infants and toddlers are natural explorers. They have a desire to make sense of their world. They begin to notice that people, animals, and objects have different characteristics and properties. They develop familiarity with hard things, soft things, sticky things, and light things. Infants discover objects that make sound and objects that bounce and roll. They begin to

combine loose parts based on a variety of attributes, including color, size, weight, and function. Loose parts that are familiar to infants can provoke comfort, while new items may challenge them to explore new ways to discover how the world functions.

Infants and toddlers begin the process of classification by sorting loose parts into piles. At first this may be a random process; however, as children become more skilled at sorting and classifying, they eventually begin to create piles according to specific attributes. Lonzo, twenty-one months old, separates items by color: all the red wooden pegs and red tiles go together. Later on he starts to classify by texture with the silky fabrics together and the ribbed fabrics in a separate basket. The process of classification allows young children to develop reasoning and thinking skills. Older toddlers are very adept at observing and finding things that do not fit together. They notice patterns and discern differences in these patterns and use more discrimination to classify items. They may now sort the wooden pegs with the wood tiles, and they notice that they are different in color but are all made of wood. They separate seedpods from seashells and sort them into small baskets; they recognize that they are natural elements, yet one belongs on land, the other on water. As they sort and classify, they test the environment to see how it operates. In the process they learn new ways of interacting with both the environment and the objects within.

The Power of a Muffin Tin

Teacher Sara places colorful bottle caps, recycled from gallon jugs of bubble solution, into clear tempered glass jars for the toddlers to see and use. Mathew, who is the first to arrive at the center, takes the jar of caps and dumps them on the floor. He begins to line them up in no particular order. Sara quietly sets a muffin tin near the caps and steps back to observe. Mathew looks at the muffin tin and places a bright pink cap inside one of the cups. He proceeds to place a different colored cap in each mold until all the caps have been arranged in the tin tray. His interest for sorting and classifying continues as he starts to sort colorful hair scrunchies. His classification ability becomes more complex throughout the week as he mixes the scrunchies with the bottle caps. He discerns that they are different yet have one characteristic in common: color. It is amazing to see how the combination of loose parts and a muffin tin become an open-ended puzzle that allows Mathew to explore multiple sorting and classifying combinations.

Ethan exclaims, "No!" as he approaches the colored circles displayed on the shelf. He dumps all the circles on the floor and starts sorting them into same-colored containers. It is apparent that circles placed in contrasting-colored containers disrupts Ethan's ideas of classification. He proceeds to change the circles to same-colored containers and places them back on the shelf in a different (maybe more coherent) arrangement.

Children begin to compare size as they investigate big and little metal spoons.

Part 4
Instrumental Exploration

It is crucial that the child discovers as much as possible on his own. If we assist in accomplishing every task, we deprive him of the single most important aspect of his development. A child who achieves things through independent experimentation acquires an entirely different kind of knowledge than does a child who has ready-made solutions offered to him.

—EMMI PIKLER
PEACEFUL BABIES—
CONTENTED MOTHERS

Banging and Pounding

Pushing and Pulling

Inserting

Twisting and Rotating

Instrumental exploration is characterized by the use of an object as a tool to produce an action, such as when a child bangs, taps, or pushes an object against another to produce sound or movement (Casby 2003a). Infants and toddlers gain further insight into how objects work, both separately and together, through instrumental exploration. They make loose parts into tools to accomplish tasks, such as when Adam used a sifter as a ball carrier. Through instrumental exploration of loose parts, young children learn concepts of causality and the relationships of force and motion.

Instrumental exploration typically begins with the investigation of a spoon, the most common tool children first use and master. Eventually young children manipulate spoons in different ways; they pass the spoon from hand to hand, place it in a dish, and sometimes use the spoon to stir in slow circular motions, pretending to make soup. The entire time, they are problem solving and exploring a variety of ways to use the spoon to meet their needs. The spoon has now become a multipurpose tool. Through engaging in instrumental exploration, children learn to use tools to solve more complex tasks. Mathew, thirty-two months old, sees a ball that is stuck between the platform and wall and out of his reach. He uses a large serving spoon as a tool to extend the length of his reach and release the ball from its stuck position. Tools thus serve as extensions of children's limbs and enhance the efficiency with which skills are performed.

Instrumental exploration gives infants and toddlers the opportunity to discover causality or how a specific action creates a reaction. Addy, twenty-two months old, and Samuel, thirty months old, work to create a ball run using black tubing. Addy tosses a ball into a black tube, but the ball stays inside the tube. She looks inquisitively and then without hesitation finds a nearby crate. Samuel helps place the crate underneath the tube to elevate it. Once again they place a ball in the tube, and this time the ball rolls out. Addy has figured out how to use the crate as a tool to prop up the tube and create a ramp. When toddlers grasp the concept of causality, they begin to make predictions about the way objects relate to each other in space. This type of exploration allows children to relate events and actions. They build patterns of expectations about how objects and people behave and interact and how tools help them solve problems effectively.

With intentionality, teachers can support young children in exploring the relationships of force and motion. They can provide opportunities for infants and toddlers to push and pull loose parts. They can encourage children to move and rotate wheels and spinners.

CHAPTER 10

Banging and Pounding

When infants and toddlers bang on drums with sticks or pound wooden dowels into clay with mallets, they gain gross-motor skills and muscle strength, and discover that they can make intriguing sounds. As their gross-motor skills increase, children begin to exhibit more outwardly oriented movements, such as holding on to a dowel and using it as a tool.

They become incredibly mobile and gain in instrumental abilities, which include using one object to act upon another. For instance, infants and toddlers can hold an object in each hand and bang them together or take a wooden mallet and pound a peg into a board. Young children make inferences about new objects and how they function, such as how wooden spoons can be used to eat and also to create sound by hitting a wooden bowl. Children are intent on exploring objects from every angle, including batting and pounding items into other objects.

When young children bang or pound objects, they test the multiple possibilities the object offers. "What will happen when I use this spoon to bang a pot?" These types of exploratory questions seem to drive their play. Infants and toddlers delight in the realization that as they bang one object with another they are instrumental in making different sounds. When they bang and pound one object into another, children are acting like scientists exploring what objects can do and what they can do with an object (Gopnik, Meltzoff, and Khul 1999).

One of the benefits of providing loose parts for children to bang is the development of gross-motor skills. Sixteen-month-old Leonardo kneels in front of the wooden salad bowl and uses a wooden spoon to bang. He starts to bang slowly. As he listens to the sounds, he begins to add more force into each bang. He is using his upper body strength each time he bangs on the wooden bowl. Leonardo stands up and goes around the circle of wooden bowls and bangs on each one with all his strength. Teacher Sharla notices that he uses more force when he bangs the large bowls and less strength with the smaller bowls. Leonardo is not only using his gross-motor skills, he is testing his muscle strength as he adjusts the force used to bang on each bowl. Loose parts that engage infants and toddlers in banging or pounding can support more purposeful and intentional play behavior while allowing them to learn to use and control their muscle strength.

Toddlers can create rhythmic patterns by banging with loose parts. Adam, twenty-two months old, approaches the sound garden and hits the metal lids with a spoon. He bangs once on the first lid, twice on the second lid, and three times on the third. He repeats the pattern a few times. He then modifies the rhythmic pattern by banging twice on the first lid, once on the second, and four times on the third. Through instrumental exploration of rhythmic patterns, Adam is gaining concepts that he will be able to later apply when he explores reading and writing. For instance, when infants and toddlers bang using a soft to loud pattern, they gain an understanding that they will use later when they learn there is a systematic relationship between letters and sounds.

How Loud Can I Bang?

Julian and Jesenia are sitting on the grass outdoors. Their new ability to crawl and sit has opened new opportunities to explore. The teachers have placed a variety of colorful plastic containers on the floor. They observe as Julian starts banging the containers with his hands. Jesenia watches intently then picks up a wooden spoon from a canister nearby and begins to pound the containers with it. She laughs at the sound and turns to choose a larger container. Julian turns to see where the sound is coming from and watches Jesenia as

she continues to bang using the spoon. Julian reaches for a wooden spoon and begins to bang all the containers with it. He brings his ear closer and listens with eager attention as he bangs with delight. This is the perfect example of the importance of giving young children the opportunity to explore loose parts together. Without knowing it, Jesenia has taught Julian a new skill.

The pestle grinds corn kernels and cocoa mulch with every striking blow. Each one produces a different sound and scent.

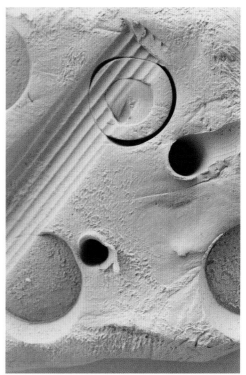

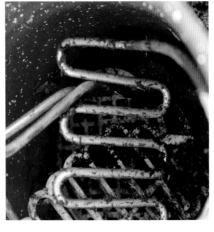

Pound, pound, pound. Children use large muscles to pound potato mashers into the mud.

Rebecca grasps the wooden mallet and rhythmically pounds golf tees into the porous round of palm tree. Then her interest shifts from the hammering sound to grasping the golf tees and pulling them out.

CHAPTER 11
Pushing and Pulling

Loose parts such as tubes to pull or boxes to push support young children's coordination, cognitive understanding of the properties of objects (such as the use of force), and an understanding of one's own physical capacities. As infants and toddlers practice more complex instrumental skills, they engage in pulling and pushing objects. They enjoy pushing a box up a small ramp or pulling a rope behind them. In this process they learn that some objects can only be pulled while others can only be pushed.

As infants explore their physical capacities, they begin to push themselves to a standing position by using an object to gain stability. Julian crawls to a wooden box containing blocks. He holds on to the edge of the box and pulls himself closer. He unfolds one leg and then the other. After a few attempts, he propels himself to a standing position. He has learned that objects such as boxes can help him accomplish the task of standing. The next day as he uses the box to stand up, he takes a step and realizes that he is pushing the box. He goes on to push the box as he takes a few more steps. He turns around and smiles at his teacher, Sharla, who delights in this new accomplishment. Julian explores pushing other boxes, large wooden bowls, and carpet tubes. He uses more force with some items and less with others. He is learning about his own physical abilities to push the objects to move them. As they further develop their skills in pulling and pushing, toddlers enjoy pushing boxes, crates, and even tables to learn about friction and to test their own strength.

In the process of pulling and pushing, infants and toddlers learn that there are specific forces that cause items to move, change directions, stop, and start. They also gain understanding of their body's capacity to exert force. They recognize their own abilities; they take risks and explore new items they can push, adjusting their physical abilities accordingly. Once infants become more adept at walking, they begin to pull loose parts behind them. As Lonzo, twenty-one months old, pulls a paint roller behind him, he requires more sophisticated balancing skills; he has to keep his hand behind him while walking. He attempts to look back to see what is happening to the paint brush he is pulling. This requires complex coordination in order to achieve the task.

Toddlers can use their thinking and physical skills to solve complex problems. They are capable of creating and acting on a plan of action to achieve a task or goal. Providing a variety of loose parts that toddlers can push and pull will support their ability to problem solve. Ian pushes a table to move it to another side of the room, but the rug on the floor gets twisted around the table legs. Ian pauses and watches; he lifts the table and pulls the rug. The table again does not move when he pushes it. He says, "This is heavy." Ian recognizes the force of friction and the use of his own physical strength to move an object.

I Have to Pull Harder

A group of toddlers start exploring toilet plungers placed in a large container filled with a thick mixture of cornstarch and water. When Lisa, the teacher, set out the exploration earlier in the morning, she was concerned that the toddlers would not be able to pull the plungers out of the mixture. She tested the exploration multiple times and had a hard time pulling the plungers herself. Lisa reflected with the other teachers, and they concluded that the plungers would still be an engaging exploration for the children. The teachers had no expectations as to the outcome and wanted the toddlers to be able to manipulate the plungers and cornstarch mixture freely. What happened was delightful and a big surprise. As the toddlers attempted to pull the plungers, the plungers got stuck and were hard to pull. The mixture created a suction that was hard to break. The children tried pulling, shaking, and mov-

ing the plungers, unsuccessfully at first. Through multiple attempts, Adam pushed the handle all the way into the mixture, bending the plunger. This caused the suction to break, and he easily pulled out the plunger. The other toddlers observed Adam's movements and began to imitate them. They had figured out how to pull the plungers out of the mixture, and they repeated the action over and over. Yoli discovered that as she pushed the plungers into the mix, they made a squishy sound. This triggered the children's laughter, and they pushed the plungers forcefully into the mix. The exploration was a success, and the problem solving and discovery were further evidence of young children's ability to think critically and to test their hypotheses until they find a solution. They are true scientists.

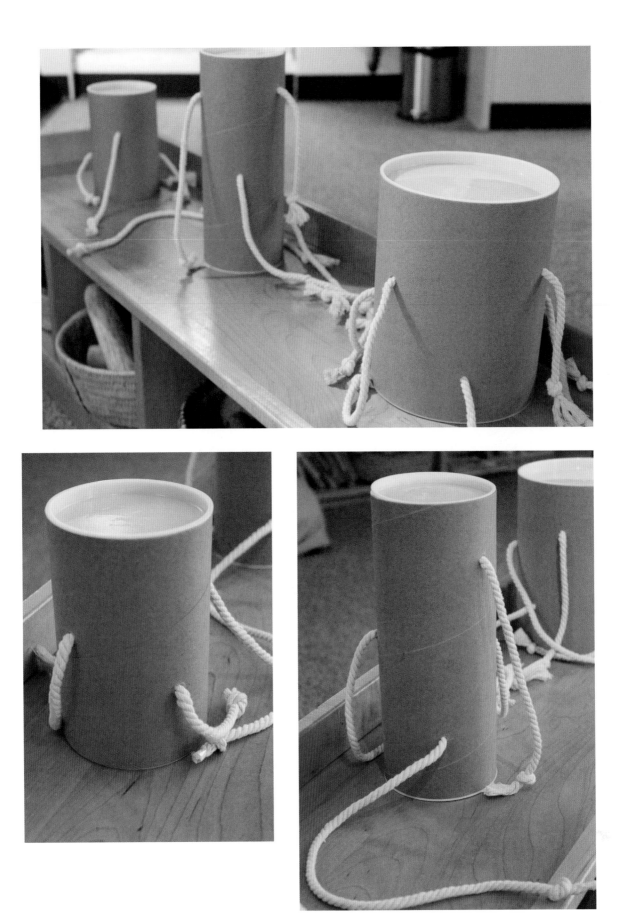

Micco pulls on the rope until it stops. He keeps pulling and is curious as to why it won't come out any further.

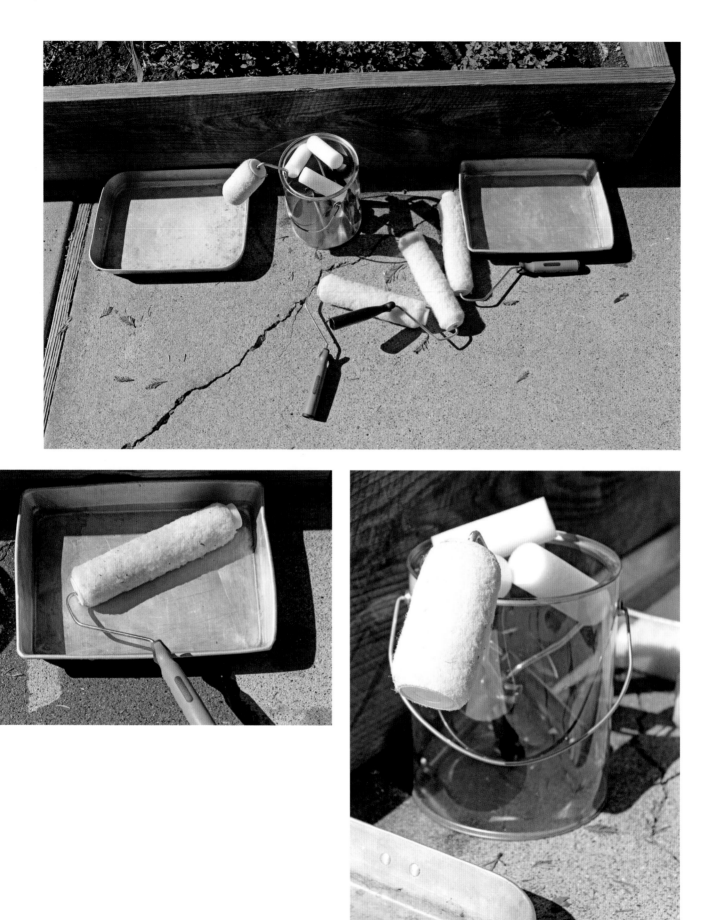

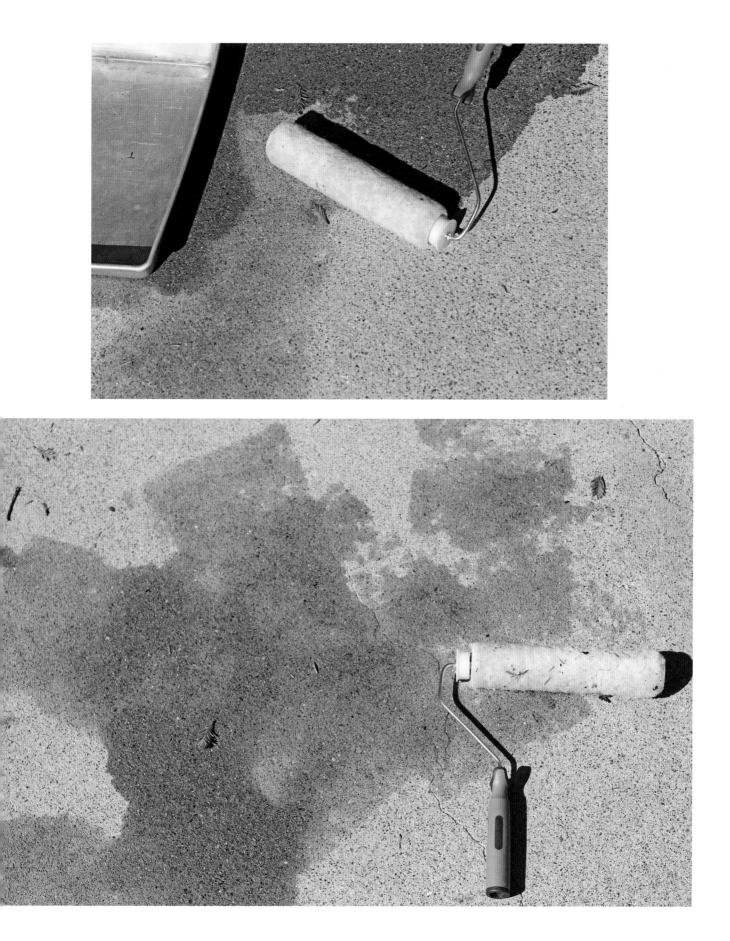

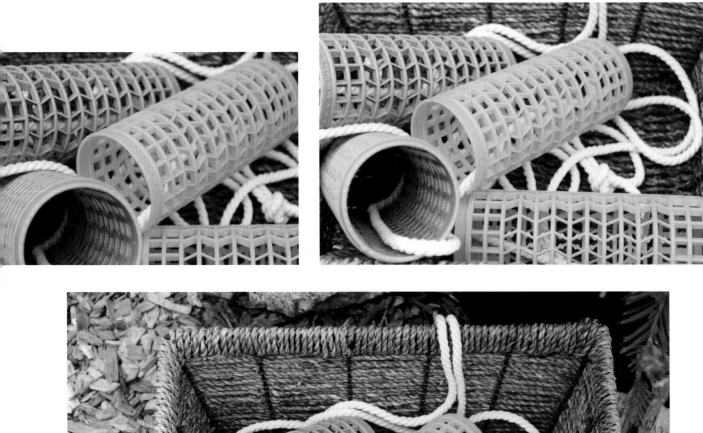

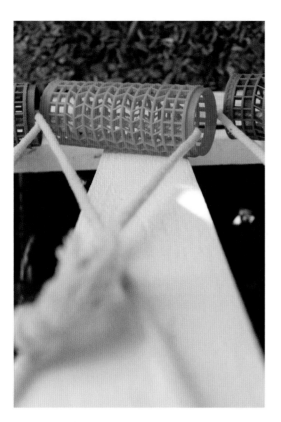

Saige enjoys pulling a yarn spinner tube, tied to a rope, behind her. She often stops to see what the tube is doing. She walks faster to see if the tube spins faster. She pushes the tube down a slide and laughs as she sees it rolling down. She pulls the rope, using a lot of strength, and brings the tube back up the slide. In this instrumental exploration, Saige is gaining knowledge of force. How much strength is needed to pull and push a tube? She is exploring motion as she measures how fast the tube rolls when she walks or runs.

CHAPTER 12

Inserting

Young children enjoy exploring novel objects and inserting loose parts into all kinds of spaces. Inserting offers them the opportunity to explore concepts of measurement and problem solving, and it supports the development of their perceptual-motor abilities. When infants and toddlers insert an object into another object or space, they begin to develop an understanding of measurement and size: "This peg is too big to fit inside this tube." A simple inserting task offers children the opportunity to problem solve and develop more complex systems of thinking. Through a series of repetitive patterns, such as inserting pieces of fabric into a weaving loom, young children develop memory, which they apply to subsequent ideas and investigations.

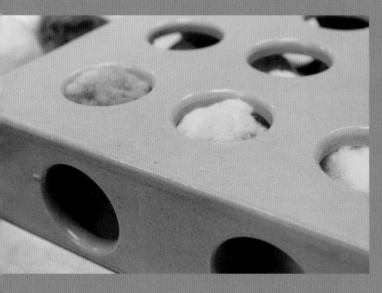

Inserting requires children to imagine and see multiple perspectives about space, size, and dimension. For example, in order to insert an object into a hole, children need to understand how a two-dimensional hole in an object is related to the object, which is three-dimensional. Nariah, thirty months old, first inserts large pom-poms into the holes of a wooden box. Next she discovers how pipe cleaners fit into the holes of a colander. Her first attempts are challenging, but with persistence and practice she becomes skilled at inserting the pipe cleaners with ease. She moves to inserting different-sized wooden dowels into containers with holes of varied size. She explores inserting thicker dowels into bigger holes and notices they fit and sometimes go through the holes. She then tries to insert a thick dowel into a smaller hole and realizes it does not fit. She tests different dowels until she finds ones that fit into the various-sized holes. She has learned about size, thickness, and circumference of objects.

As infants and toddlers gain more skill in inserting, they recognize that sometimes they have to rotate items in order to make them fit. They engage in problem solving as they test different hypotheses on what makes objects fit together. They begin to plan and pursue specific goals. In this process young children are learning about their own spatial abilities and their own capacity for solving problems. A further challenge is how to retrieve a loose part that has fallen inside a container. This requires children to adapt a reverse concept of insertion. They now have to adjust their thinking to retrieve the item. Nine-month-old Jesenia shakes a container in an attempt to remove a plastic hair roller. Leonardo, sixteen months old, inserts tongs into a container to retrieve an item. This shows a progression in the understanding of space and of two-dimensional and three-dimensional relationships.

Ian Discovers Hollow Blocks

Ian, thirty-three months old, is particularly interested in inserting loose parts into different spaces. He will insert a stick through the open fence, or he will insert different objects inside plastic bottles. He goes on to figure out how to get inserted objects out of bottles. Today Ian discovers a hollow block near the natural tree cookies and begins to insert

the cookies into its opening. A new game of inserting begins. As he inserts a tree cookie into the hollow opening, the cookie gets stuck and won't go in. This is when Ian notices that some of the tree cookies are bigger than others. He lines up the tree cookies to see their size, then takes one tree cookie at a time and tries to fit each one inside the block. If a tree cookie does not fit inside the hollow open-

ing, he places it back in the container. He does not give up until he successfully finds a tree cookie that fits. Ian is focused and intentional and spends a long time engaged in inserting activities, even when they present a challenge.

Yoli meticulously inserts a piece of ribbon into the weaving loom and manages to thread the ribbon through a few holes. As Yoli inserts another piece of ribbon, Mathew runs and gets inside the A-frame loom. He takes the ribbon that Yoli has inserted and pushes it out a different hole. Yoli stops, watches as the ribbon emerges, and then takes it and passes it back to Mathew. A wonderful collaboration begins, and both Mathew and Yoli benefit from this newfound relationship.

Inserting pipe cleaners into a metal colander can be quite tricky for older infants and toddlers. The children discover that it is easier if the colander is turned upside down.

CHAPTER 13

Twisting and Rotating

As infants and toddlers become more adept at manipulating objects, they begin to recognize the different ways objects function. They rotate objects to analyze them from different angles. In this process, they are combining their visual acuity with their motor skills to gain knowledge of the three-dimensionality of objects. They enjoy spending time rotating and turning objects to explore movement. Their exploration is productive and deliberate. Their newly developed ability to coordinate their wrists, fingers, and palms engages them in tasks such as screwing

and unscrewing jar lids. When Ian, a toddler, turns doorknobs or manipulates a nut onto a bolt, he adjusts his grip and changes his body's position to increase his leverage. These tasks require strong understanding of speed, weight, strength, and force.

A wall with a variety of wheels to spin can help children gain knowledge of how items rotate and how to manipulate them. Rotating schema often engages toddlers in energetic actions, and young children will frequently run and walk in circles, spin in place until they fall, or twist ribbons, scarves, and ropes. Spinning their bodies helps young children's brains develop by stimulating the vestibular system (sensory information about motion, equilibrium, and spatial orientation), thus increasing a sense of balance and equilibrium. Offering infants and toddlers provocations that increase the complexity and challenge of rotation and circularity can further support schema learning and development.

Ethan, thirty-two months old, enjoys objects that he can twist and rotate. Handheld eggbeaters, flour sifters, salad spinners, and pepper mills challenge his physical skills. With practice and repetition, Ethan becomes skilled at turning and manipulating each item. He is focused on the power of his own actions; he is interested in making things happen and seeing how objects behave as he rotates them. He describes the action by saying, "Goes round," thus making a connection to language as a vehicle to explain his actions. Ethan's fascination with rotation suggests cognitive structure that informs his actions. He transfers his knowledge of how things rotate to other areas of play, such as turning a lazy Susan while holding a crayon to make circles on a piece of paper. When young children make the connection that it is their action that causes an object to rotate, they learn that there is a functional dependency relationship between their actions and the way the object rotates (Athey 2007).

Rebecca's Story: Round and Round She Goes

Rebecca, thirty-two months old, is fascinated with drawing circles, spinning, and things that rotate round and round. In the morning she draws circle after circle, covering a full sheet of paper. She meticulously fills in each circle with paint, using the same circular motion, and later uses her finger to make circles in sand on the light table. She is often seen twirling around, watching her skirt fan out with each turn. At the water table, Rebecca pours water into a water wheel. She watches intently as the water cascades into the wheel, causing the wheel to spin in circles. On other occasions, she investigates the rotation of an eggbeater as she cranks the handle to make the blades go round, and she is excited when small pinecones fly off the revolving lazy Susan. She uses circular motions as she pretends to stir a concoction of dirt and water and softly sings a *whiz, whiz* sound as she twists a nut onto a bolt. Rebecca's captivation with rotation extends to dramatic play as she pretends to drive a bus. She straddles the log, sits, and grasps the old wheel that is secured to it. She drives the bus, making the wheel spin round and round as she turns corners. Her investigations are deeply satisfying and engaging, and in each instance her focus is on the spinning movement.

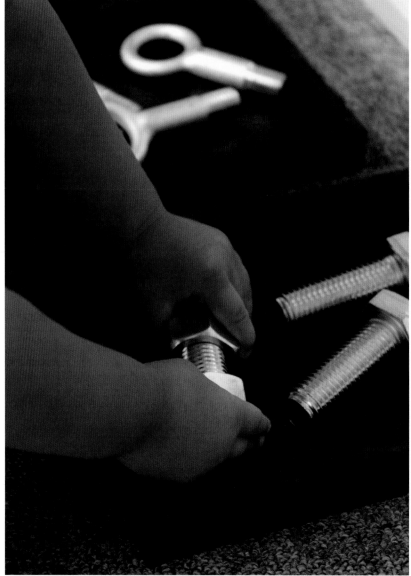

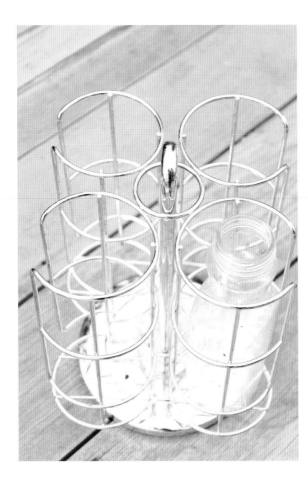

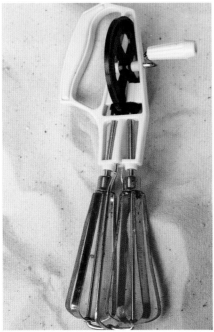

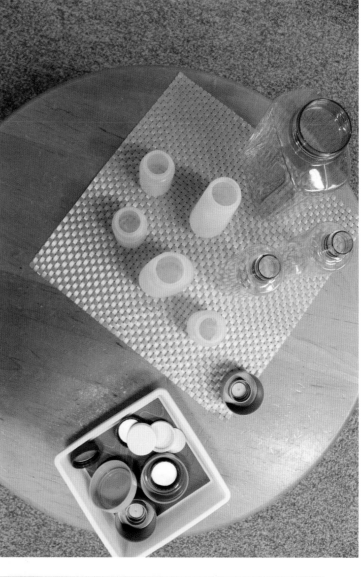

Adam's interest shifts from matching caps and bottles to twisting and untwisting the caps. To his surprise, he finds out that the next cap he tries to screw on a bottle will not turn. He looks at the cap, analyzes the bottle, and after a second attempt, he looks for a different cap. This time, when he places the cap on the bottle and starts screwing it on, he notices it is working. Adam twists the cap on, carefully using rotating motions. He discovers that he is able to screw the cap onto the bottle even when rotating the bottle instead of the cap.

Julian and Jesenia are fascinated with the spinning rotation of tops—a loose parts find from a medical supply company. Julian uses his thumb while Jesenia uses her hand to spin the tops.

Part 5
Locomotion

Balancing

Swinging

Climbing

Children play
beautifully on their own.
They do not need to be
taught how to play.

—MAGDA GERBER AND
ALLISON JOHNSON
YOUR SELF-CONFIDENT BABY

Transporting

By the end of their first year,

infants increase their ability to move from one place to another and to freely explore their environment. This new capacity is known as *locomotion*. Through locomotion, infants encounter new opportunities for learning, as they move, change location, and recognize the relationship of their bodies to other objects within space. Movement provides infants and toddlers with the ability to make connections and increase in social, emotional, cognitive, and physical capacity. Locomotion is a skill that develops over time and within caring and engaging environments. With practice, young children begin to acquire a sense of orientation and the ability to problem solve as they traverse different terrains. This is derived from their understanding of spatial relationships with objects and challenges in the external environment. As they move, infants and toddlers use their sense of hearing, sight, and touch, as well as their vestibular and proprioceptive senses. The vestibular sense gives children sensory information about motion, equilibrium, and spatial orientation. The proprioceptive system assists in children's ability to sense stimuli within their bodies regarding position, motion, and equilibrium. These systems send sensations to the infants' and toddlers' muscles and joints to guide their ability to maneuver encountered obstacles.

Locomotion offers infants and toddlers entry into the world of social relationships. As they start crawling, infants reach to touch other infants in their space. They may crawl next to each other or simply sit and observe what the other is doing. Locomotion expands their world since they are now able to more actively pursue their interests and join other children in simple play exchanges. As they continue to gain in locomotion abilities and start to walk, older infants and toddlers socially engage with other children and adults by imitating their actions. Curiosity propels them to explore objects and spaces and encourages close connections with others through hugging, holding, and social interactions.

Young children gain a strong sense of competence as they accomplish locomotion tasks. Nine-month-old Jesenia attempts to climb the small step that leads to the toddlers' room. First, she crawls up to the step and places both her hands on it. She attempts to lift one leg over the step but rolls backward. She never gives up, and after a week she manages to climb up the first step. She turns around and gives the teachers a big smile. Jesenia has a strong sense of competence that now allows her to investigate other opportunities to climb.

As young children gain physical ability, they go through a diverse repertoire of movements and actions. They begin in infancy by discovering their hands and understanding that they can control their movements. Children then progress into more coordinated efforts, such as pulling, rolling, sitting, standing, crawling, and eventually walking. Each locomotive discovery motivates more complex interactions within their environment. They practice and repeat each movement until mastered. Locomotion requires young children's flexibility and adaptability to their surroundings. Loose parts in the environment, which offer variability and novelty (such as large tree cookies, different stepping stones, and large tubes for climbing), help children adapt their physical and locomotive abilities to different terrains. Bryce, twenty-two months old, has recently started walking and now walks back and forth on the wooden balance beam in the grass and rock garden, and he steps from one large tree cookie to the next.

Locomotion is closely connected to cognitive development and problem-solving abilities. As infants and toddlers experience a variety of surfaces and challenges, they gain in their capacity to adapt to new challenges. They also grow in their understanding of how their body moves in space and what they need to do to accomplish more complex tasks. Loose parts offer young children challenges to problem solve: "How do I get to the next tree stump? Do I sit and crawl, or do I walk?"

CHAPTER 14

Balancing

Infants and toddlers need to master balance as a precursor for whole-body movement and locomotion. Young children's ultimate goal when they move is to reach a desirable object. In this process, they need to avoid obstacles and surfaces that stand in their way. This requires them to see an obstacle, maneuver themselves around the obstacle, and successfully reach out for their desired object. An integration of all their senses, including vision, touch, hearing, and vestibular, is necessary in order to balance.

Kinesthesis, or the position and movement of our body parts, along with the understanding of how we use our bodies in space, helps infants and toddlers make meaning of the power they have in their environment. Balance and equilibrium offer infants and toddlers information about where their bodies are in relationship to other objects in space. Balance and equilibrium also work together by coordinating children's movement in relationship to an external object in the environment. Once young children develop more balance and equilibrium, they start to engage in more sophisticated interactions, such as balancing a ball on a large spoon as they walk to deposit the ball into a container. They begin to push large items together or climb steps. Providing infants and toddlers with a variety of surfaces to walk on, such as large tree cookies, tiles, and rugs held by sticky tape, supports them in enhancing their balance and equilibrium. They learn how to balance their bodies in new ways as they traverse over different surfaces and successfully climb over obstacles. Over time and with practice, children begin to recall the skills that are needed to accomplish different tasks. This is the beginning of abstract thought.

Samuel Balances the Tree Cookies

Samuel, an older toddler, is moving "food" into a pretend house created out of wooden planks. After carrying several small pinecones and stones into the structure, he goes back to the plank that holds natural loose parts and pretends the items are more food. Addy and he are really hungry and need a lot of food. This time he stops in front of the tree cookies and looks at them closely. He crouches down, picks up one tree cookie with each hand, and stacks the two pieces of wood on top of each other. He proceeds to add three more cookies until he has created a high, straight tower that stands almost as tall as his chin. He is now presented with the challenge of how he will transport this tower of food to his house. Samuel places his hands at the bottom of the stack to pick up the entire

tower at once. He clutches the tree cookies and balances them under his chin. He walks slowly and carefully in a hunched-over position for a few feet until he loses his grasp and the tree cookies come tumbling down. His actions required a tremendous amount of thinking, problem solving, and coordination.

Diego is testing his balance by walking across various logs placed throughout the environment.

Ian delights in seeing how many balls he can balance in a sifter. He moves them around the yard and smiles as he manages to keep them in the sifter.

The plank suddenly shifts as Seth is halfway down the ramp. A surprised look appears on his face as he extends his arms to keep his balance. He walks faster until he gets to the end of the plank and jumps off. Kaitlin is next to tackle the ramp. She goes up and down a few times, increasing her speed with each new turn. Maya, a small toddler and a risk taker, comes over to the ramp. She goes to Juwan, looks up, and extends her hand for Juwan to grasp. She takes steady, careful steps up the plank.

A variety of stepping-stones presents interesting challenges for infants and toddlers to explore their perceptual-motor coordination.

CHAPTER 15
Transporting

As young children gain in motor abilities, the transporting schema commonly emerges. They enjoy moving loose parts from one area of the room to another. As they begin to treasure specific objects, they may store them in their pockets or place them in a bag to carry with them. The schema of transporting gives us insight into infants' and toddlers' line of thought and intentions.

The transporting schema is characterized by children's interest and curiosity in moving loose parts. Transporting objects using carts, bags, baskets, and even pockets requires balance and equilibrium. Teachers can support the need for transporting by providing a variety of loose parts infants and toddlers can move themselves. Baskets with handles and a variety of bags and boxes can be placed in the environment to facilitate moving and transporting items. This allows young children to gain control of their environment as they rearrange loose parts in a way that makes sense to them. Transporting schema is also related to the concept of having and ownership. When a child places a valued object in a backpack or inside a pocket and carries that object with him, he is demonstrating his wanting to own and protect that object. Maya, twenty-six months old, transports her backpack from home and keeps it next to her all day. When her teacher asked, "What is inside?" she replied, "Home." Having access to resources from home and using them in her own way seems to offer Maya a sense of comfort. Maya also seems to know the value of specific loose parts and will store new toys to trade or share as a way to make friends.

Infants and toddlers also enjoy being transported by others, including children and adults. Large wooden boxes with wheels and handles can encourage children to move each other within the learning environment. Large baskets or buckets offer young children spaces to climb into and be transported by an adult or other children. Transporting schema is a precursor to mathematical thinking. When infants and toddlers transport loose parts, they are acquiring the understanding of quantity (How many tree cookies can I add to the basket?); weight (How heavy is the basket with the tree cookies?); and number sense (I can carry a rock with each hand).

My Bag of Cedar Rings

Makayla, an older toddler, carries a small bag with her wherever she goes. She is often seen placing pebbles inside baskets and moving them to another side of the room. In her classroom, she prefers the black purse with handles and looks for it every morning as she comes into the program. Cheri, the teacher, knows the importance of supporting Makayla's transporting schema, so she offers baskets, containers, purses, and bags that are easy to carry around. She also knows that in their need to transport, young children will move items to different locations, and she has set up her environment accordingly. Cheri is not surprised when she sees Makayla transport cedar rings from the stacking table to outdoors. She knows that Makayla enjoys transporting and has also seen Makayla engage with other children in transporting loose parts around the environment. What is truly

amazing is Makayla's sense of knowing how many objects she is carrying in the bag. Though she is unable to count the cedar rings in her bag, she instinctually knows if one was taken from the bag.

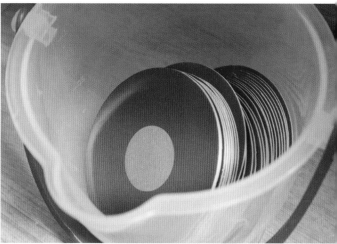

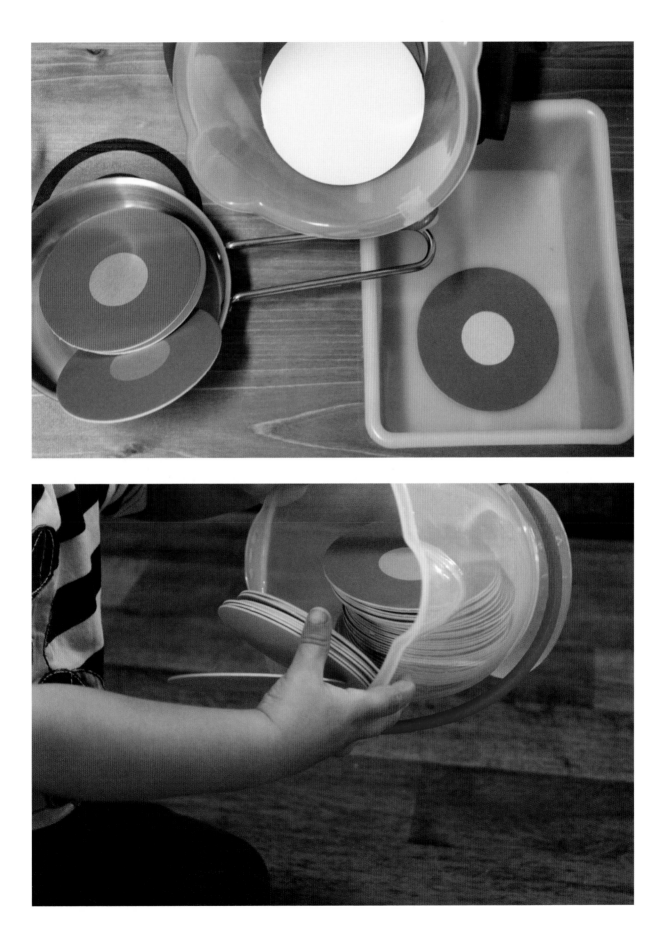

In the morning, as the toddlers are outside enjoying the fresh air, Cheri places a large container of multicolored balls next to a structure that has elevated tubing for rolling the balls down to promote trajectory. Addy has a different idea. She is busy separating green balls from all the other colored balls. She calls the balls "apples" as she puts only the green balls into a large can. She transports the balls, balancing the can, over to the playhouse and sets them on the table. She then moves the balls out of the house and around the yard, stopping here and there. She eventually places the can of balls on the back of a tricycle and starts pedaling to take them home for her family. When Jenna asks her, "Addy, where did you buy the apples?" Addy responds, "Over there in the supermarket," as she points toward the large tub in the yard. Addy turns in her tricycle seat and reaches down behind her to grasp an apple from the bucket. As she pedals off, she takes a pretend bite out of the apple.

Saige fills a bucket with metal chain and transports it everywhere she goes around the yard. She sets it down as something captures her interest and then picks it up again and carries it with her as she moves on to her next discovery.

CHAPTER 16
Climbing

As soon as infants begin crawling, they start to look for opportunities to climb. Once they are able to walk, their climbing skills increase. In the process of learning to climb, young children acquire some important skills. They learn their own boundaries and how high they are willing to climb. They recognize what feels safe and what does not, and they make decisions accordingly. They test their limits and learn to take risks. Infants and toddlers are persistent and learn to climb by trial and error, developing a strong self-competence. Climbing requires focus, awareness, and confidence. Climbing is fun and sometimes daunting, giving young children a great sense of joy, excitement, and accomplishment.

When children begin to crawl and explore their environment, they discover places to climb. Spaces and surfaces that are challenging encourage infants and toddlers to test their bodies in different ways. An obstacle course created with burlap sacks filled with sand can create interesting paths for young children to climb and maneuver as they crawl. Micco, ten months old, through trial and error has learned to climb on pillows. He is now ready for a bigger challenge. When Sharla, the teacher, takes him outside to play, he immediately crawls to the climbing structure and begins to crawl up one side that has tree cookies built into it. On his first attempt, he slides down. The next time, he holds on to the tree cookie to pull himself up. Through trial and error, he has conquered a new challenge. The environment allows Micco to feel safe, and he is willing to test other places to climb. Sharla encourages his interest and offers him new possibilities for climbing, such as pillows and ramps.

Infants' interest in climbing grows as they transition into toddlerhood. Climbing gives toddlers the opportunity to develop and exercise various systems in their bodies. Stretching to reach the next level builds upper-body, grip, and arm strength. Pulling to climb a slide or a ladder builds leg strength and coordination. Young children do this as they test their limits and climb higher structures. Jacob, who is just starting to take a few steps, is fearless. He approaches a large tube that has been propped to create an incline. He places both hands on the edge of the tube and lifts his foot over the edge. He pushes up and easily climbs into the tube. He sits inside and smiles, enjoying his accomplishment. The moment Jacob starts to walk, he takes more risks. He climbs up the stairs to the slide and onto the first level of the geodome structure on the playground. He instinctually knows how high he can climb and trusts his body to guide him. As infants and toddlers explore their new moving abilities, they need an environment that engages them in physical exploration both indoors and outdoors.

Seth's Obstacle Course

Juwan trusts the abilities of the toddlers in her care and is constantly finding ways to challenge them. She notices that the older toddlers are taking more risks with their climbing, so she finds a way to transform the climbing structure on the playground to stretch their ability. She secures a large plastic drainage tube to the structure's steps, creating a tunnel to climb. This simple change is fascinating to the toddlers, who explore the different ways of getting to the top of the structure.

This morning the older toddlers build an obstacle course with Juwan by placing two large bicycle wheels in front of the large tube. Seth is ready to take on this new challenge. He jumps in the first tire, then the second, and begins to pull himself into the tube. He places his hands on the tube's edge, throws his left knee up, then his right, and uses his arm and leg strength to climb all the way up. When he emerges from the tube at the top of the structure, he stands up. His sense of accomplishment is evident as he puts his hands up in the air and laughs.

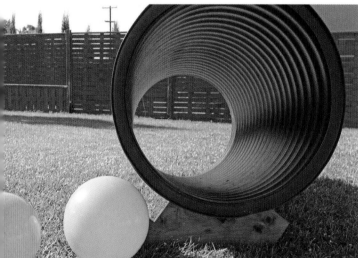

Saige, a skilled walker, is now testing her climbing skills. She easily climbs into the tube and joins Jacob inside. They sit together for a few minutes and then turn to climb down. Jacob crawls to the tube opening and turns onto his tummy. He slowly moves one foot to securely touch the ground, gets his other foot down, and pushes himself off the tube. Saige takes a different strategy. She sits on the edge of the tube and puts one foot down and then the other. This demonstrates that young children are capable of successfully accomplishing even tasks that present risk.

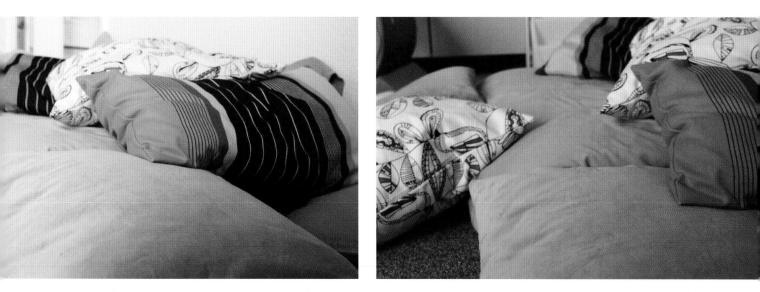

Pillows and cushions provide Micco with an obstacle course to climb inside the classroom.

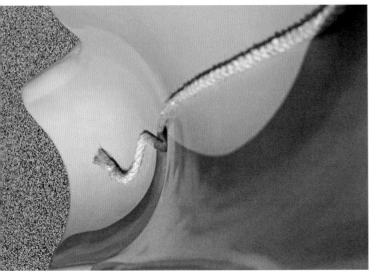

Recognizing that older toddlers need risk taking, Juwan secures a rope to the top of the slide. It takes tremendous strength, power, and determination for children to pull themselves all the way to the top of the slide.

CHAPTER 17
Swinging

Swings are disappearing from many parks and play yards, yet they are significant in early childhood play. Providing swings made from loose parts such as tires, chairs, and barrels supports infants' and toddlers' development. Swings are an important part of promoting physical development while they offer young children opportunity to augment their senses and understand gravity. Swinging supports sensory integration, the process in which the brain organizes and interprets the information provided by the senses. Sensory integration serves as a foundation for complex learning and behavior. Swinging also engages and supports the vestibular system, improving children's ability to balance. The following are just some of the many benefits swings offer infants and toddlers.

Young children require a coordinated effort to propel a swing to move. Toddlers need to move their legs in a specific action while establishing a rhythmic motion. A sense of timing is essential to make the swing move, so practice makes perfect. The more children have the opportunity to swing, the more they are capable of establishing a rhythm to move the swing back and forth. Swings help older toddlers strengthen their core and increase their coordination and balance.

Swinging takes a lot of balance in order to sit independently while holding on and pumping legs to make a swing move. Learning to balance while sitting on a swing offers toddlers a different challenge and sensation than walking and running. Standing on a swing takes courage and the capacity to take risks, even with the close supervision of an adult; taking such a risk is linked to knowing your abilities and recognizing your limits. Balancing in a swing requires a toddler to exercise her cognitive abilities: "How can I hold on, make the swing move, and not fall off?"

Swinging engages both infants and toddlers in addressing their fears: "I am okay and I won't fall." It promotes emotional well-being. There is nothing more calming and soothing than quietly swinging. Swings can serve as refuge for young children who want to think, ponder, and reflect. Swings are also perfect for encouraging socialization. Toddlers can build friendships as they swing next to each other. They can push each other and teach each other to swing, gently developing empathy and the ability to care for others. Swings also help children develop independence. Once a child learns to swing, she is capable of sustaining the motion independently while acquiring a sense of accomplishment.

When young children swing, they spend time imagining and thinking about what interests them. Swinging gives infants and toddlers the opportunity to imagine what it feels like to fly or how high they can swing. Imagination is an important part of developing critical thinking skills, and swinging allows children the opportunity to dream, explore, and test their own abilities and capacities. It also allows them to test their limits in a safe and supportive way.

Niqui and the Swing

Niqui, a young toddler, is transitioning into a new environment. Every morning when she walks into the outdoor environment, she observes how a group of children gather around a wooden disk suspended from a tree branch, which has been repurposed as a swing. She stands quietly and waits until the older toddlers leave the swing. She approaches the swing and attempts to get on it. This is a difficult task, since the swing keeps moving. She walks away and spends the morning walking around observing other children at play. The teachers know she is adjusting to a new environment and invite her to join other children at play, 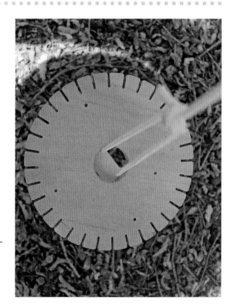 which she hesitantly does. Every day Niqui returns to the swing and attempts to climb and sit on it, until finally one day she accomplishes her goal. She sits on the swing and smiles. Mariana, one of the older toddlers, approaches the swing and gently pushes Niqui. The swing begins to move, and a new friendship is formed. After that day, Niqui plays with other toddlers and more actively explores the environment. The simple swing made out of loose parts has helped Niqui through a difficult transition into a new program.

Who would have thought that a chair makes a perfect swing for children to enjoy?

The preschoolers in this learning environment used their imagination and creativity to engineer a swing. They connected a rope to a plank and the geodome, making an innovative swing that the toddlers enjoy.

Part 6
Action

Trajectory

Throwing

Pretending

Constructing

The infant's curiosity and interests determine
what activities the infant needs to engage in
and what he will create, learn, and enjoy.
—DAVID ELKIND
THE POWER OF PLAY

In the first two years of life, young children are more physically active than at any other time in their lives. Toddlers in particular are more interested in play that includes large-motor activities. Since they are now accomplished walkers, they begin to test their large muscles in more complex ways. Toddlers are in a constant stage of motion as they practice newly learned skills, such as jumping, climbing, rolling, throwing, and constructing. They are testing their strength and making meaning of how their actions relate to their newfound physical abilities. In this process they learn that certain conditions are necessary for specific actions to take place. For example, as toddlers build a tower with crates, they are measuring their strength and gaining knowledge of the rules of physics.

Children's understanding of the world grows as they gain body awareness and are more capable of monitoring their bodies in space. Parallel play becomes more prevalent, and older infants often engage in frisky active play. They may roll side by side, copy each other as they throw a ball, or climb on each other. As they engage in action play, infants test ideas and hypotheses, or find answers to questions about the function of loose parts. This period of time can be challenging for teachers and families. However, with understanding and knowledge that there is purpose in young children's actions, they can support children's exploration in safe, yet engaging ways.

Active exploration or experiences in which infants and toddlers combine the use of their body with an object increases children's ability to think and reason. This happens whether or not the anticipated result occurs. For example, a large ball rolled down a big tube will come out on the opposite end. Young children are often surprised by this development. How does the ball enter the tube on one side and roll down to exit on the opposite side? As infants and toddlers make meaning of an unexpected action, they commence a new level of learning. In other words, they make sense of this new information within the context of previous knowledge.

Action-driven exploration of loose parts also stimulates learning and development by engaging infants and toddlers in large-muscle play that not only supports children's physical abilities, it also allows them to gain social awareness and respect for people and objects. They recognize that the way they use their bodies will cause a response from peers and adults. When toddlers run to greet one another, they have to regulate their strength and body movement. They learn to adjust their movements so as not to knock another child to

the floor. They transfer this information when they toss, drop, or roll loose parts. For instance, they know they have to adjust the force used to roll a wooden spool down a ramp or it will roll over the ramp's edge.

Action play provides a vehicle for young children to develop emotional thinking. They learn to interpret their own movements and gestures as well as those of other people. For example, when an infant or toddler is ready to throw a ball, an adult smile sends the message "Go ahead." An adult frown, however, says, "Please wait." Eventually children are capable of applying this emotional thinking to different situations they encounter throughout their lives, such as reading people's body language before they answer a question or join a conversation.

Action play engages children's intellect, as infants and toddlers have to figure how things work, how their body works, and how events happen. As Jonah, an older toddler, rolls a tree cookie down cove molding, he needs to consider the molding's incline and where the tree cookie will land. He makes adjustments as he analyzes how to make the cookie travel further. This requires both cognitive and scientific abilities. Action play also includes pretend, or symbolic, play. This type of action play engages young children in active representation of moments and interactions with people and objects in their environment.

Young children exhibit different schemas of play as they explore their environment. These are clearly connected to both thought and movement. Schemas allow infants and toddlers to make sense of how objects function and gain the ability to gather, recall, organize, and process information, and their thoughts and behaviors. In this way they gain knowledge and understanding of the many concepts the world offers them. For example, when children transition into a new environment, they may spend time enveloping themselves with a blanket or hiding under a table. This enveloping schema allows them to express their feelings about the new place while creating a sense of safety for themselves.

In this part we cover concepts about throwing and trajectory. We recognize that they are both part of the same play schema. However, each concept is discussed separately to differentiate the ways in which children demonstrate the schema in their play. A free dropping and throwing representation of the schema is shown in the throwing chapter. Ramps are used as vehicles to roll and move objects as part of a more complex representation of the schema in the trajectory chapter.

CHAPTER 18
Throwing

Infants and toddlers are budding scientists as they delight in exploring what happens when an object is thrown. They seem to be guided by the question, "What happens when I open my hand and the object I am holding falls to the ground?" They test this concept over and over and carefully observe the effects of gravity. At a certain point, they begin to experiment with the idea of not only dropping an object but also throwing it. This is an exciting new skill that they will test repeatedly. They realize that the loose part thrown always comes down; it may bounce or roll or splat on the floor. Curiosity is the driving force behind throwing loose parts. It is the engine of intellectual learning. Young children are persistent and willing to explore and discover new items and ways of throwing them. In doing so, they are learning about weight, gravity, strength, and distance.

Since throwing is a common schema, or repetitive action, in young children, allowing them to throw different loose parts, such as felted balls and other soft objects, in a safe and controlled environment gives infants and toddlers the ability to test their own knowledge. They can figure out that a metal spoon will make a loud noise when it lands on the floor, while a pom-pom will make almost no sound. They learn that a ball thrown against a variety of empty oatmeal cans will make one or more of the cans fall. By throwing, they are also integrating visual perception as they aim an object to hit a specific target. As they learn more about their own physical abilities and the properties of the loose parts, they become more intentional in their actions. Part of their enjoyment comes from reliving the experience multiple times until they are satisfied and ready to move to the next exploration.

Adults can incorporate loose parts that allow children to explore the throwing schema safely. Providing large plastic crates that children can build with and knock down or empty oatmeal containers they can knock over with a ball will fulfill the urge to throw in a productive and purposeful way. Often older infants and toddlers use trajectory schema to engage in social interactions. They throw a beanbag to another child as an invitation to play. Observing young children in these interactions can offer a deeper understanding of their intent and thinking.

How Loose Parts Fall

Throwing is a trajectory schema that is often seen in older infants' and toddlers' play. It is a child's unstoppable urge to explore causality, force, gravity, and strength. Throwing schema involves active play and engages Bryce, twenty-two months old, to further understand his own abilities and how loose parts work. Bryce is often found running outside and building towers that he can knock down by throwing a ball. When he throws a soft ball across the yard, he notices that it does not move as fast as a hard plastic ball. When Bryce throws a loose part from the play structure, he is learning the fundamental principles of gravity. As Bryce throws soft loofahs up in the air, he is exploring his own strength. The teachers know that throwing is not malicious or a mistaken behavior, but instead  is a strong need to learn more about the way objects in the environment work. They are constantly finding ways to support Bryce's throwing schema by placing loose parts in the environment that he can safely throw.

Teacher Janna has observed that Adam, twenty-two months old, is constantly throwing blocks, cars, soft rubber animals, and puzzle pieces. Rather than constantly saying no, she places a basket of soft loose parts in the small loft to support his need to throw. Upon his arrival in the morning, Adam sees the basket of objects. He runs up the loft ramp and starts throwing balls over the loft's side to the pillows below. Ariana, who is new to the program, watches intently. Adam throws a ball to her, which lands at her feet. A game starts: Adam throws one ball at a time and Ariana attempts to catch it. This moment supports Adam's throwing schema while helping Ariana feel more welcomed into her new environment.

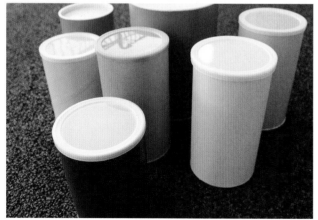

Painted oatmeal containers offer children a colorful target to knock down with balls.

The children discovered that wrapping a ball inside a scarf makes the scarf go higher when thrown into the air.

CHAPTER 19
Trajectory

Trajectory is a very common schema and one that infants and toddlers often display. "An interest in trajectories is characterized by an ongoing fascination with things moving through space, both vertically and horizontally. It may be objects, or the child's own body" (van Wijk 2008, 21). This schema begins with a simple love of dropping objects from their high chairs. Infants are fascinated by the sound and way items drop, and what happens to the objects once they land on the floor. As children get older, they show an interest in things that move. Adam is a very active toddler, who is often seen moving around the room and bouncing or rolling different loose parts found in the environment. He watches as a ball rolls down a ramp, curious about the object's movement. Ariana is also a very energetic toddler and loves going up and down the tree stumps in the outdoor environment. She jumps and is constantly testing how far she can go. Her trajectory interest is with her body's ability to climb, jump, and move fast. Both children are learning about height and speed, yet their interest is different. Adam is learning the concepts of up, down, on, and off. Ariana is learning about concepts of distance and speed. Play schemas such as trajectory are strengthened through action-oriented exploration, movement, and investigation. In an environment that offers loose parts, enriched opportunities and endless possibilities for learning abound.

Exploring trajectory is an important part of young children's learning and the acquisition of scientific and mathematical thinking. For example, as infants and toddlers explore loose parts that roll, they gain knowledge of shape and function. Once they can differentiate between a cylinder and a cube, they begin to roll only the cylinder down a hill. This type of physical knowledge helps young children make more complex mental relationships while they play. They invent more problems to solve and engage in more purposeful exploratory play, which loose parts can support. Large carpet tubes and cove molding can serve as ramps that can be adjusted to provide different inclines and give children the opportunity to observe how an object moves. Large boxes offer older infants and toddlers the opportunity to climb, move across, and crawl under the boxes. Water walls created with a variety of funnels and tubing give them an opportunity to openly explore movement, flow, and trajectory.

Marlysa and Alvin: Roll, Alvin, Roll

With teacher Cheri's help, the older toddlers build a complex ramp in the grass area outside. They begin by placing two pieces of cove molding on top of a barrel. They release a few balls and watch how far they roll. Samuel places a blue can at the far end of the cove molding to capture the balls as they hit the grass. The preschool children join the play and help the toddlers build a more complex structure. They prop a black open tube on top of tree stumps, logs, and crates. As they are building the ramp, the tube keeps falling off the tree stump. Marlysa, twenty-two months old, runs and picks up a heavy rock and places it at the end of the tube to hold it in place. The older children clap for Marlysa, and Cheri delights in the toddlers' abilities and capacities to problem solve. The children are now ready to test their structure by rolling different types of balls down the ramp.

Alvin, twenty-one months old, joins the play and rolls a few fabric balls cautiously down the ramp. The balls make it to the end of the ramp and stop before they hit the grass. Marlysa runs over to the crate of balls and care-
fully selects an orange plastic ball. She stands at the beginning of the ramp and releases the ball. This time the ball rolls all the way and lands in the grass, far away from the tube. Marlysa retrieves the ball and hands it over to Alvin. She runs to the opposite end of the ramp and lies down on the floor. She yells to Alvin,

"Roll." Alvin releases the orange ball and it stops at the end of the ramp. Marlysa continues to observe as Alvin rolls other balls down the ramp. They both laugh as they notice that there are five balls stuck at the bottom of the tube. Marlysa gets up, and Alvin rolls one more ball, which pushes the other balls into the grass. Marlysa and Alvin both clap in delight.

Teacher Sara asks Ian, "Which ball do you think will go farthest?" Ian predicts the ball on the right. He watches as balls simultaneously roll down the cove molding inclines and smiles when his prediction is correct. He then uses another strategy as he moves one end of the cove molding higher. Even as a toddler, Ian is engaging in engineering and complex mathematical learning as he explores trajectory by creating ramps.

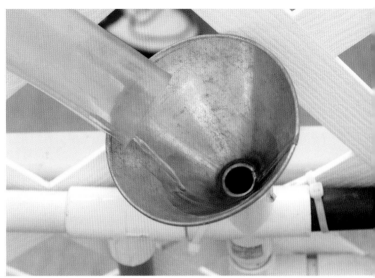

Jacob enjoys watching pinecones roll down a small plastic slide.

CHAPTER 20

Pretending

Pretend or imaginative play emerges around twelve to eighteen months of age and serves as a way for young children to make sense of situations that go on around them. Pretend play requires the ability to transform objects and actions symbolically. For example, a toddler picks up a spoon and a cup and pretends to eat. Through imaginative play, young children begin to understand that when they say good-bye to a parent who is going off to work, that parent will come back to pick them up at the end of the day. Older infants and toddlers will pretend that they are off to work while they leave their doll behind. They may also re-create a visit to the doctor by using a bamboo stick to give a stuffed animal a shot. Since their language is limited, playing is really the best way to work out their feelings. As children get older, they gradually begin to engage in more imaginative and complex play. They can turn boxes into trains or cars and pretend they are going on a trip. They enjoy making forts out of blankets and pillows.

As young children become more engaged with pretend play, they will begin to use loose parts to represent something else. Addy, twenty-two months old, takes a green ball, brings it up to her mouth, and exclaims, "This apple good." Loose parts support infants' and toddlers' emergent ability to use symbols. As explicit memory (permanent memory) develops, children will engage in simple rituals and representations that they observe taking place in their lives. They will wrap themselves in a blanket and pretend to be sleeping or feed a stuffed animal, pretending it is a pet. Observe and listen to young children engaged in pretend play; it is apparent that they are involved in social interactions that include negotiation, perspective and role taking, imagination, and planning.

Through pretend play, children start to play cooperatively. They take on other people's roles and invite other children to join, as they take turns pretending to be superheroes, using scarves as capes. Taking others' roles allows young children to see different perspectives. Thus they begin to develop a better understanding of other people's thinking and respond with empathy.

A Place for the Jungle Animals to Play

Kenton, Maya, and Antoine are toddlers entering the stage of pretend play. They enjoy spending time under the shade of a beautiful tree. They bring a variety of logs, tree cookies, and rocks to their tree, which they arrange in interesting configurations. They create pathways with the rocks and slides with the logs by propping them on top of tree stumps. Kenton brings a basket of jungle animals over to the area and begins to take out one animal at a time. Antoine joins Kenton and places the tiger coming head first down the slide. Antoine says to the tiger, "Slide." Maya runs over to the mud kitchen and brings a wooden bowl with water. She nods to Kenton and exclaims, "They thirsty." Kenton balances different animals on the rocks and branches. She watches carefully as the lion falls to the ground. She picks it up and places it on a log, and holds on until the lion is perfectly balanced.

Toddlers seem to be engaged in their own pretend play, yet they find ways to socialize and engage with one another. Their play sequence is simple and still reveals each one's thinking. Antoine is active, so when he places the tiger on the slide, we know that he is exploring his own abilities. Maya is caring and empathic. She is constantly helping other children. This is represented in her pretend play when she brings a bowl of water for the animals to drink. Kenton is thoughtful and a researcher. She is constantly testing new hypotheses. This is revealed in her approach to balancing the animals on different surfaces.

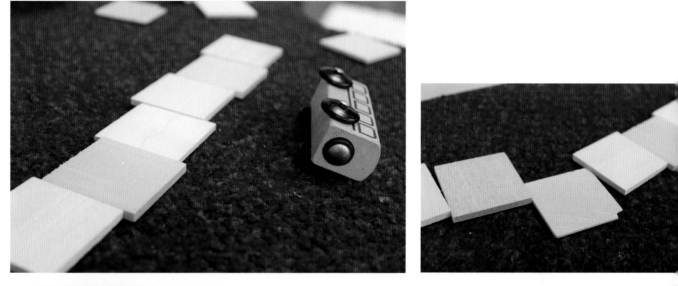

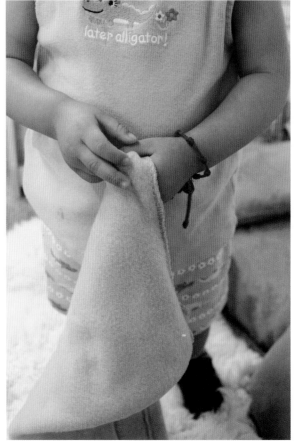

Arianna tucks her pig, and then herself, into bed.
Later she carries around the pig while she goes shopping.

In order to encourage pretend play, teacher Cheri often sets out new provocations with loose parts for the children to explore. Today she sets up an outdoor station to wash and dry cloth napkins. Samuel is focused on making sure the clothespin secures the napkin to the clothesline. This is challenging, so he works at it until he manages to successfully hang the napkin.

CHAPTER 21
Constructing

By the age of two, children engage in constructive play, which is a more focused and sustained play that involves the use of objects to build something. They move from exploring objects in a repetitive and simple way to this type of more purposeful play. When toddlers start constructing, they will investigate loose parts. They learn how to hold them, carry them, and discern how heavy they are. They experiment with building a tower using plastic cups and knocking it down. Eventually their constructions are more sophisticated and representative of their play. Loose parts allow young children to use their creativity to invent towers, bridges, train tracks, and other items from their imagination. As children construct, they ask questions, wondering: "What will happen if I put this box on top of another box? How tall can I build a tower?"

As children construct, they have a sense of purpose. Ian, thirty-three months old, loves trains and spends time every day using loose parts to create train tracks. He uses cove molding to make a ramp and rolls the train down. Later he makes a representation of a train track by lining up wooden squares. He is experimenting with different objects, finding combinations that work and do not work. He is testing possibilities and using different materials. Construction gives young children a sense of accomplishment and empowers them with control of their environment.

Construction develops children's imagination and problem-solving skills, and allows them to discover new building possibilities. As older infants and toddlers construct a pasture for their animals or a house for their dolls, they are learning important spatial relationships and mathematical concepts. Children can take more risks and engage in building more intricate structures with experience and when there is no right or wrong way to construct. Ian and Yoli, both thirty-three months old, use small crates to build. At first they only place one crate on top of another crate. Later they start building a taller tower. Their construction becomes more sophisticated, and they eventually build an enclosure. They are learning about size, comparing objects by matching them, and counting how many crates they need to complete the enclosure. When the tower tumbles down, they are gaining an understanding of how cause and effect change their goals. Construction is a social activity that brings children together, and Ian and Yoli are often seen spending time building together.

From House to Boat

The older toddlers at Cheri's family early child care and education program used loose parts to make a house for Otis, the desert tortoise. They worked hard to create a complex and well-balanced structure. The next day, as the children come out to play, they see the house and the different loose parts. Addy goes over to the loose parts, takes a basket to the house, and exclaims, "My house." Samuel joins her and brings other loose parts over to what is now their house. They start placing some tree cookies on top of the structure, and it begins to fall apart. Addy and Samuel then start to rebuild the structure. With some verbal prompting from Cheri about where to place the wood planks, they attempt to re-create the house structure the way the other children designed it. As it often happens, the house keeps falling apart. Addy and Samuel take a large piece of wood cut into triangles with a base at the bottom. They attempt to balance it, yet it keeps falling. In an attempt to make the wood piece stand, Addy sits on one of the triangles. She notices that it is now balanced, so she says, "Look is a boat." Samuel comes over to join Addy, as he exclaims, "A boat, a boat." Their play has shifted from constructing a house to building a boat. With Cheri's trust, the children are now using large loose parts to construct innovative and imaginative structures.

Nicholas is particularly interested in constructing tall towers. He piles small crates as high as he can before they topple over.

Yoli discovers new loose parts that nest on top of each other and foster her interest in building towers.

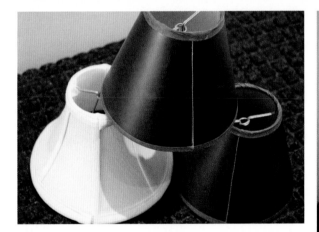

References

Athey, Chris. 2007. *Extending Thought in Young Children: A Parent-Teacher Partnership*. London: Paul Chapman Publishing.

Bijvoet–van den Berg, S., and E. Hoicka. 2014. "Individual Differences and Age-Related Changes in Divergent Thinking in Toddlers and Preschoolers." *Developmental Psychology* 50 (6): 1629–39. http://dx.doi.org/10.1037/a0036131.

Casby, M. W. 2003a. "The Development of Play in Infants, Toddlers, and Young Children." *Communication Disorders Quarterly* 24 (4): 163–74.

Casby, M. W. 2003b. "Developmental Assessment of Play: A Model for Early Intervention." *Communication Disorders Quarterly* 24 (4): 175–83.

Daly, L., and M. Beloglovsky. 2015a. "Introducing Loose Parts to Preschoolers." *Teaching Young Children*. 9 (1): 18–20.

Daly, L., and M. Beloglovsky. 2015b. *Loose Parts: Inspiring Play in Young Children*. St. Paul, MN: Redleaf Press.

Gerber, Magda. 2013. "The Best Toys for Babies Don't Do Anything." Magda Gerber, Seeing Babies with New Eyes. www.magdagerber.org.

Gopnik, Alison. 2009. *The Philosophical Baby: What Children's Minds Tell Us about Truth, Love, and the Meaning of Life*. New York: Farrar, Straus and Giroux.

Gopnik, Alison, Andrew N. Meltzoff, and Patricia K. Kuhl. 1999. *The Scientist in the Crib: What Early Learning Tells Us about the Mind*. New York: HarperCollins.

Harper, Susan. 2004. "Support Schemas in Areas of Play." *Playcentre Journal* 121 (Spring).

Katz, Lillian. 2015. "Lively Minds: Distinctions between Academic versus Intellectual Goals for Young Children." Jamaica Plain, MA: Defending the Early Years.

Kálló, E., and G. Balog. 2005. *The Origins of Free Play*. Budapest, Hungary: Pikler-Loczy Association for Young Children.

Maguire-Fong, Mary Jane. 2015. *Teaching and Learning with Infants and Toddlers: Where Meaning-Making Begins*. New York: Teachers College Press.

Meade, Anne, and Pam Cubey. 2008. *Thinking Children: Learning about Schemas*. Berkshire, England: Open University Press.

Nicolson, Simon. 1971. "How NOT to Cheat Children: The Theory of Loose Parts." *Landscape Architecture* 62:30–34.

Piaget J. 1952. *The Origins of Intelligence in Children*. New York: International Universities Press.

Shonkoff, Jack P., and Deborah A. Phillips, eds. 2000. *From Neurons to Neighborhoods: The Science of Early Childhood Development*. Washington, D.C.: National Academy Press.

U.S. Consumer Product Safety Commission. "The Safe Nursery: A Booklet to Help Avoid Injuries from Nursery Furniture and Equipment." Washington, DC: U.S. Consumer Product Safety Commission. Accessed August 9. www.cpsc.gov.

van Wijk, Nikolien. 2008. *Getting Started with Schemas: Revealing the Wonder-full World of Children's Play*. New Zealand: The New Zealand Playcentre Federation.